100 YEARS
100 TREASURES

A Celebration of Suffolk Churches

For the
GANZONI FAMILY

whose steadfast and continuing support
sustains Suffolk churches

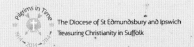

The Diocese of St Edmundsbury and Ipswich
Treasuring Christianity in Suffolk

Front cover: *Bronze statue of St Edmund at St Edmundsbury Cathedral by Dame Elisabeth Frink RA (1930-93)*

Back cover: *Wooden cross at Blyford All Saints from Captain Walter Day's grave in Flanders, where he was killed in 1916 at the age of 31.*

This window was specially commissioned to celebrate the centenary of the Diocese of St Edmundsbury and Ipswich by the Friends of Wortham Church. Designed by local artist Jane Durant, it features scenes from Wortham village, as well as St Edmundsbury Cathedral tower and the old priory ruins to represent the constant renewal of the church.

Poppies appear as a symbol of remembrance with the date 1914 linking the diocesan centenary with that of the start of World War I.

Dedication of the window took place on 14 April 2013 by the Bishop of St Edmundsbury and Ipswich the Rt Revd Nigel Stock.

Published by the St Edmundsbury and Ipswich Diocesan Board of Finance, St Nicholas Centre, 4 Cutler Street, Ipswich, Suffolk IP1 1UQ

ISBN No. 978-0-9927031-0-3

Foreword by the Rt Revd Nigel Stock,

Bishop of St Edmundsbury and Ipswich, 22 October 2007— 21 October 2013 *

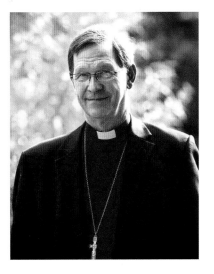

THIS book is an important part of the celebrations of the creation of the Diocese of St Edmundsbury and Ipswich in 1914. The diocese was created out of the Dioceses of Norwich and Ely as a deliberate move on the part of the Church of England to minister directly to the historic county of Suffolk. Of course, that year saw the start of the World War I which was to leave its mark on the whole country. Indeed, the first Bishop of St Edmundsbury and Ipswich, Henry Hodgson, lost his son Noel in the Somme offensive in 1916.

The churches in all their communities hold so much of the history of the locality. Inevitably the lists of those who fell in the 1914-18 War are very much a feature of churches up and down the country. This book is an illustration of some of the many ways in which our church buildings are interwoven with community life and that very much remains the case today.

The churches in Suffolk must be among the finest in the land. In size, they range from the grand and impressive such as Long Melford, Lavenham and Blythburgh, to tiny gems such as Shelland and Thornham Parva. They all remind us of our history within the county. Whether seen as places of worship, repositories of beautiful artefacts, evidence of inspired engineering, or architectural features in the landscape, they cannot be ignored by anyone who is in the least bit curious about our history.

So in celebration of the centenary, I invite you to explore as many of these buildings as you can. The 100 treasures in this book give you a starting point but, as those who put together these 100 treasures can no doubt tell you, it could just as easily have been 200 or 300 treasures.

Enjoy what you see in these pages which have been chosen by a wide range of people hoping to inspire, delight, and perhaps surprise you. I hope that they and the churches that contain them, will give you a flavour of the 100 years that have passed since the foundation of the diocese and point to all the possibilities for the future for the life of the Church in our diocese.

* Prior to his translation to be Bishop at Lambeth.

FIRST WORLD WAR CENTENARY

A donation from the sale of this book will go to the Royal British Legion in recognition of the sacrifices made in WW1 which broke out in 1914.

As the nation's leading Armed Forces charity, the Royal British Legion spends $1.6 million a week, or $84 million a year on vital welfare work, providing social, emotional and financial care and support to serving and ex-Service people and their families.

Approximately 9.5 million people in the UK are eligible for the Legion's support and the charity aims to serve those in need, today and for the rest of their lives.

With over 340,000 members, the Legion is one of UK's largest membership organisations. It provides comradeship to all who support the aims of the charity, and gives the wider community a way to express a sentiment of solidarity, pride and friendship with those who have served.

The Legion works to promote the interests of the Armed Forces community through high profile lobbying of government and other policymakers. Heard at the highest levels, it is able to influence new legislation and policies.

The Royal British Legion is also the national custodian of Remembrance, ensuring that the sacrifices made on behalf of the nation are honoured and remembered. This is most poignantly demonstrated through the Two Minute Silence.

If you would like more information about The Royal British Legion in Suffolk please contact Suffolk@britishlegion.org.uk

'100 YEARS, 100 TREASURES'

WELCOME to '100 years, 100 treasures' to mark 100 years of the Diocese of St Edmundsbury and Ipswich.

Our 478 churches contain far more treasures than we could ever hope to cover in a publication like this. We have therefore not tried to do the impossible but to ask parishes themselves what they most treasure in their own churches. The result is that some of the treasures you might have expected to see are not included. Instead we aim to show you treasures that might be new to you in churches you may not have thought of visiting before. They include fascinating memorials, intricate woodwork, vibrant stained glass and beautiful flint flushwork in which our diocese reigns supreme.

Neither are we confined to the 15th century when so much money from the wool cloth trade was lavished on our churches. We have tried to include something from every period represented in this diocese – from the Anglo Saxons and Normans through to Medieval times and on to the Victorians - right up to the 21st century. The only criterion for churches to be included was that they should be unlocked and welcoming to visitors whether or not they are manned.

Well known churches expert and author Roy Tricker has traced the history of the diocese from 1914 to the present day, an absorbing and fascinating read before you get on to the treasures themselves..

You will find a fold out map at the back of the book to enable you to locate the treasures in your area and to help you plan a day out discovering places you had not previously thought of. The glossary at the end of the treasures is there to help those who are not familiar with some of the traditions of the Christian Church and if you are keen to learn more, we have included suggestions for further reading.

We have tried to make this little book accessible to all ages. It may serve as a history resource for schools, a pocket book for travellers, or a companion for pilgrims. Our historic churches are among the finest in Europe and built to be awe-inspiring. They are also places for simple prayers, quiet reflection or for remembering loved ones.

We hope you will be uplifted by them.

HISTORY OF THE DIOCESE

by Roy Tricker

The Church convivial: Archdeacon George Hodges of Sudbury (1888-1912) and Canon Reginald Wilson (1912-23), both instrumental in the formation of the new diocese.

THE diocese of St Edmundsbury and Ipswich was legally 'born' on 21 January 1914, when 355 East Suffolk parishes were transferred from Norwich's vast diocese (of 1151 parishes and 890 parish priests), together with 177 West Suffolk parishes (the archdeaconry of Sudbury which had been part of the Ely diocese since 1837) to form Suffolk's own diocese. The documents recording the discussions, disagreements, developments and decisions over several years in the planning of the new diocese make fascinating reading. Plans made in 1889 to rearrange the dioceses of Norwich, Ely and St Albans had come to nothing and in 1904, discussions began in earnest about the creation of the new diocese

for Suffolk and another for Essex (then part of St Albans diocese, which had a population of 1.25 million).

Many meetings took place between 1905 and 1913 to fix the diocesan boundaries, which hopefully would match county boundaries, but from the start there was a 'possible reservation' about the deanery of Lothingland - the finger of north-east Suffolk which juts into Norfolk and then included Gorleston. Later the then north Suffolk deaneries of Wangford, South Elmham and North Dunwich (which included Southwold, Beccles, Bungay and Halesworth) also asked to remain with Norwich. In those days, when few people had cars and relied upon the railways, valid points were made about the difficulty for Lowestoft residents to travel to Ipswich to see their bishop or, worse still, to the cathedral at Bury St Edmunds, while access to Norwich was simpler and cheaper. Only at the very last minute did the Ecclesiastical Commissioners decree that although the other three deaneries were to join the new diocese, Lothingland would remain with Norwich. Lowestoft rejoiced in the local Press that 'common sense has prevailed over red tape'!

The name of the new diocese, also where the cathedral should be and where the bishop should live provoked much discussion and a little rivalry between East and West Suffolk. It was agreed in 1907 that the cathedral should be in Bury St Edmunds, that the bishop should reside in or around Ipswich and that the new See should be called the 'Diocese of Suffolk'. As no English diocese had ever used a county name, alternatives were discussed and the rather long-winded title of St Edmundsbury and Ipswich was agreed. Concern about the bishop's ink supply provoked one suggestion that his title might be adjusted to 'the Bishop of St Edmund's (Bury and Ipswich)' and that his signature could omit the bracketed bit!

St James' Bury St Edmunds was chosen to be the cathedral because (unlike St Mary's) there was room for it to be developed and extended, also because Arthur Maitland Wilson of Stowlangtoft, the patron of the living, was happy to

surrender his patron's right as a free gift. His cousin, Reginald, had arrived as vicar in 1912 and was to remain until 1923. St Mary's patrons were Evangelical trustees and it was felt that they may not be so easy to deal with, but many at St Mary's thought it unfair that they had been 'passed over'. Moreover they felt that the final decision had been hastily made at what they called a 'hole in a corner' meeting of five people in a private house, three of whom were members of St James' Church. Some Stowmarket church members suggested that since they were just about in the centre of the diocese, within easy reach of both Ipswich and Bury, and had a mighty church, they might become Suffolk's cathedral city.

Bishop Henry Hodgson, our first Bishop, enthroned in 1914 before a 1,300-strong congregation.

The beautiful Bishop's Chapel in Park Road Ipswich, designed by Henry Munro Cautley and built in 1927, mostly by local craftsmen.

Stoke Hall (situated within easy reach of Ipswich station and St Mary Stoke church) was purchased in 1909 for the bishop's residence and in 1913 plans were drawn up to duly modify it, but the new bishop disliked it and leased Parklands, a grand house in Park Road, designed by John Shewell Corder and built in 1895 for a local coal merchant. The diocese purchased it in 1920 and its beautiful chapel, designed by Henry Munro Cautley, was built and furnished (mostly by local craftsmen) in 1927.

On Shrove Tuesday 1914 our first bishop, Henry Bernard Hodgson, was consecrated in St Paul's Cathedral (with John Watts Ditchfield, first bishop of Chelmsford). Some Suffolk people were sad that Bishop Luke Paget of Stepney (the much-loved suffragan Bishop of Ipswich and rector of Nacton and Levington from 1906 -1909) was not chosen. When the 'ladies of the diocese' were asked to subscribe towards a pastoral staff for their new bishop, some argued that a car might be a more useful gift and the Revd J Milner, the ultra-protestant rector of Chilton, wrote at length about pastoral staffs being illegal ornaments in the Reformed Church!

Bishop Hodgson was enthroned on Lady Day 1914 before a congregation of 1300. The press warned that about 900 ticket-holders would be boarding trains from Bury St Edmunds railway station between 5.29 and 5.43 p.m., many on the special trains that had been provided. Less than five months later, our country was plunged into the turmoil of the First World War. Bishop Hodgson's wisdom, patience, pastoral skills and experience as a parish priest and archdeacon were ideal for the task of making a new diocese live and thrive and by 1921, when he died in harness aged 65, much had been achieved under his leadership. His successor, Albert Augustus David, had been headmaster of Rugby School. He was a gracious and godly evangelical – a people-friendly person who announced that he had 'come to learn'. Suffolk church people were indeed sad when, after only two years, he was translated to Liverpool's very urban diocese.

Under the bearded Bishop Walter Godfrey Whittingham (1923-40), the diocese had a period of reasonable stability. His obituary informs us that some of his views were excitingly ahead of his time. He was a 'champion of youth', who welcomed people attending church services in casual dress, believing that 'the dance and whist-drive were means of helping Church fellowship'; he even stated that in his personal opinion, some divorced 'innocent parties' should be entitled to re-marry in church.

Because of wartime conditions Bishop Richard Brook (1940-54) was consecrated in what was to be his own cathedral. Despite the war years, also the decline in churchgoing and reduction of clergy numbers that followed, this wise and resolute Bishop set about the task of pastoral reorganisation and regrouping of parishes, also providing new and more manageable parsonage houses. During his time Leiston Abbey was opened as our diocesan Retreat House and the very active Guild of St Edmund was formed for the young people of the diocese, who invaded Bury St Edmunds every Whit Monday for their great Youth Festival.

Under the kindly and caring leadership of Bishop Harold Morris (1954-66), the diocese celebrated its Golden Jubilee with a variety of services and events. During 1964 the beautiful Processional

Bishop Richard Brook (1940-54), with Canon William Cocks, vicar of St John's Felixstowe 1921-62.

Bishop Leslie Wilfred Brown (1966-78), who moved continents to come to the diocese and moved house during his time here.

Cross with Arrows, designed by Jack Penton, made by Hector Moore and given by the Readers of the diocese (and now kept near the Edmund Chapel in the cathedral), made its way to every parish church in the diocese and then back to the cathedral.

Bishop Leslie Brown (1966-78) came to us having done pioneering work leading to the formation of the Church of South India and had been Archbishop in Uganda. During his time we embraced synodical government, we saw the failure of the Anglican-Methodist reunion scheme, the arrival of new forms of worship, the consecration of our enlarged and transformed cathedral in 1970 and the pioneering in our diocese of the ministry of Elders in 1968. It was Bishop Brown who exchanged the Bishop's House for the more manageable 4 Park Road, Ipswich. The former is now 'Norwood', a care home run by the Methodist Church, and there is a licence agreement for the bishop and his staff to share the use of the chapel.

Each succeeding bishop has left his own individual mark for good upon Suffolk. Bishop John Waine (1978-86) brought to our diocese great energy and skill, gained from his years as a parish priest in challenging parishes, and as a suffragan bishop. Our 70th year in 1984 saw a variety of events, including a great Eucharist in the Abbey Gardens with the Archbishop of Canterbury. With Bishop John Dennis (1986-97) came the introduction of Ordained Local Ministry, the ordination of our first female priests and the setting up our link with the diocese of Kagera in Tanzania. The episcopate of Bishop Richard Lewis (1997- 2008) saw the emergence of sad disagreements in the Anglican Communion and his loving and inclusive leadership encouraged us all to think, pray, listen and love a little more deeply, wherever our sympathies lay. In his six years in Suffolk, our tenth bishop, Nigel Stock's dedication in getting to know and to be known at the grass roots of the diocese and his open, approachable and positive nature have greatly encouraged Suffolk church people to be confident in their faith and to look hopefully to the future.

The first Bishop of Dunwich, appointed in 1934 to share the diocesan bishop's work, was Maxwell Homfray Maxwell-Gumbleton; he was also Archdeacon of Sudbury and rector of Hitcham (where his bishop's and churchwardens' stalls may still be seen). Bishop Clement Ricketts, who succeeded him (1945-55), was rector of Dennington where his pastoral staff (a Cotswold shepherd's crook) is preserved. Bishop Thomas Cashmore (1955-67) was a large and dignified figure and a dynamic preacher, known by those who dared as 'Uncle Tom' and by others as 'the purple-headed mountain', in recognition of the purple Canterbury cap which he habitually wore.   Bishop Clive Young was the ninth and longest-serving Bishop of Dunwich (1999 – 2013) and people in our diocese and county will long remember his wisdom and kindness, also a wealth of fascinating sermons composed for a variety of occasions.

Our cathedral remains a parish church as well as the Mother Church of the diocese. It was Provost John White (1940-58) who began the long process of making the building more worthy of its cathedral status and who invited Stephen Dykes Bower to prepare the plans. The dynamic and down-to-earth leadership of Provost John Waddington steered the cathedral's life from 1958-1976. The new north-west porch and library were dedicated in 1960 and eight bays of the cloisters were built the following year, followed in 1963-70 by the transformation of our cathedral, as the soaring quire, transepts and side chapels took shape. The 21st century has seen the great central tower rising 150 feet into the sky and many other developments where the skills and talents of our own times have made

The great central tower of the 21st century contrasts with the Norman tower of the old abbey.

Provost John Waddington (1958-76), under whose dynamic leadership the Cathedral was transformed.

talented woodcarver, who ran woodwork classes for his parishioners and whose craftsmanship adorns his own church and several others in the area.

At its outset the diocese produced a monthly Diocesan Magazine. With a cover and 16 (later 20) printed pages, this ran until March 1957. It was financed until 1939 by its publisher (WE Harrison of the Ancient House, Ipswich) and then by the diocese, at a loss, with about 450 regular subscribers. It was decided to replace it by making the quarterly leaflet 'News of the Diocese' (with a circulation of 3,000 as inserts to parish magazines) into a monthly publication. This later became 'The Church in Suffolk' and is now the 'East Anglican' with a monthly print-run of over 7,500.

our cathedral a splendid and sacred place which is wonderful, warm and welcoming to all.

The clergy who have served our diocese over its 100 years have included a host of fascinating characters. Some were experts in their fields, like Dr Frederick Warren (Bardwell 1890-1922), who wrote scholarly works on ancient rites and liturgies, James Gilchrist (Dennington 1955-66) who was an authority on Anglican church plate and Algernon Ogle Wintle (Lawshall 1923-59), the skilled maker and repairer of 'tingle-tangle' barrel organs, which he frequently played on the streets of Bury St Edmunds. Archdeacon James Darling (Eyke 1893-1938) was a

The parish magazine has always been an important part of parish life. The past 100 years produced many interesting, attractive and thought-provoking magazines from Suffolk parishes. In 1959 the cathedral brought out 'Cathedral News' a new illustrated magazine, which was much on the lines of the 'Mancroft Review' – the splendid journal which the new provost had produced in his former Norwich parish. For much of the 20th century many parish magazines ran at a loss, so parishes combined forces to produce deanery or district magazines, and at various periods over the past 100 years at least 260 Suffolk parishes (half the diocese) were served by these publications. One of the largest was the

St Andrew's Felixstowe, built and furnished for conservative evangelical worship. Note what the text proclaims above the holy table.

'Newmarket & District Church News', which covered 13 Suffolk parishes and 22 Cambridgeshire ones.

The diocese has reflected the kaleidoscope of traditions which enrich the 'comprehensive school' that is the Church of England. Ipswich became an evangelical stronghold in the 19th century, with eight out of its 12 ancient parishes in this tradition which, by 1914, was also established in the town parishes of Stowmarket, Beccles, Southwold, St Mary's Bury St Edmunds, All Saints' Sudbury, 'Walton-cum-Felixstow' and in many Suffolk villages. A fascinating shrine of 20th century conservative evangelicalism is St Andrew's Felixstowe, whose foundation stone proclaims to passers- by that the church was built in thanksgiving for the rejection of the 1928 Prayer Book and the maintenance thereby in the English Church of 'the teaching of Holy Scripture and the Principles of the Reformation'. Bishop Hodgson inherited several well-established Anglo catholic centres, not only in the major towns, but also vibrant centres of 'Country Catholicism' at Barsham, Capel St Mary, Chevington, Kettlebaston, Shipmeadow, Swilland and elsewhere.

When the minutiae of churchmanship were more contentious than now, troubles occasionally occurred. The ritualistic

13

'goings on' at Capel St Mary were given a good airing in the newspapers in 1927, when a Consistory Court ordered the removal of 28 'popish' articles from the church. Hundreds of flyers were handed out in Ipswich before Ash Wednesday 1923, advertising a Protestant lecture which would expose the 'Amazing Superstition at St Bartholomew's – Blacking of faces for the Remission of Sins – and to witness against 'Holy Water, Holy Candles and Holy Soot'!

Some clergy spent most of their ministry in their little corners of Suffolk, as did the saintly Canon Arthur Waskett (Hundon 1929-81), who had little time for many of the workings of the 'Church bureaucratic', but had a worldwide reputation as an intercessor, healer and spiritual director. Canon Geoffrey Grant came to Levington and Nacton in 1964 and is still there, with five parishes now in his care. The record goes to the bearded and staunchly protestant Edward Falconer, vicar of Old Newton (1890-1948), who was to become England's oldest working cleric. He lived to preach his 6,000th sermon and died a month after he retired at the age of 98. Waldringfield has had over 150 years unbroken succession of Waller rectors: Henry Waller arrived in 1862, his son Arthur succeeded him in 1906, followed by Trevor in 1948 and John in 1974. At nearby Felixstowe, Canon William Cocks arrived as vicar of St John's in 1921 and stayed for 40 years. In 1937-38 he presided over an electoral roll of 719, a Mothers' Union with over 250 members, a bible class of 115, a Men's Society of over 70 and a total of 14,510 acts of communion.

In 1914 the diocese was graced by nearly 500 'working' medieval churches (and over twenty 19th century ones) – each one an unique character, with its own beauty, interest, treasures and living history – built to inspire us and maybe even bring us to our knees. These range from some of the finest 15th century parish churches in the land to tiny and unforgettable hidden 'gems'. They show the best in craftsmanship and design, covering 1,000 years, from Saxon work (at Hemingstone, Debenham, Claydon and elsewhere) to modern and vibrant church centres like St Michael's Martlesham Heath (1991). There are remote little shrines like Badley (a mile down a largely unmade road), Langham (in a field), Hunston and Wantisden. There are little shoals of churches within a mile of each other (e.g. around Playford, Hoo and the South Elmhams) and some of Ipswich's 12 medieval churches are only yards from each other. Suffolk ranks high in the world for flushwork panelling, seven sacrament fonts, hammerbeam roofs and much else. Since the Pastoral Measure of 1968 set up a procedure for churches to close with integrity, some have retired from their active ministry as parish churches. Of these, 18 'churches (and portions of two others) are now lovingly and expertly conserved by the Churches Conservation Trust. In Ipswich, four out of the five churches in the care of the Ipswich Churches Trust have been given new and exciting leases of life. Of the other 14 or so of Suffolk's 'retired' churches, three are used regularly for Christian worship, two for community use and five have been sensitively converted into houses. In Ipswich, where the population moved from the town to the new suburbs, although seven town centre churches have closed, 14 or so (still active) suburban churches have been built during the past 170 years.

Our churches are treasure-houses of beauty and craftsmanship of many periods – the very best that people could create, because nothing but the best was (or is) fit for the House of God. This little book shows only a tiny sample of the beauty and living history waiting to inspire and amaze us in and around our churches – all created with love and skill for the glory of God and as sermons and sacraments in craftsmanship which can bring people to their knees. They have inspired generations of people over the centuries and it is our privilege to maintain them, intact and beautiful, for future generations to use and to enjoy.

Bishop Arthur Harold Morris (1954-66), who presided at the Golden Jubilee in 1964, with Bishop Cashmore, top right.

A prayer from the

VERY REVD DR FRANCES WARD

Dean of St Edmundsbury Cathedral

God of heaven and earth,

we come with thankful hearts to enjoy the beauty of your world

in building, art and glorious surroundings.

As we celebrate the craftsmanship of the centuries,

we commend the pilgrims of today

who seek to know your love more deeply in their lives.

Inspire them with the wonder of your presence

and surround them with your grace and blessing.

In the name of Jesus Christ our Lord.

THE TREASURES ...

1

A TOWER BUILT BY THE LOCALS

C15 panels at Santon Downham St Mary IP27 0TQ

This little church is set in the heart of the Thetford forest, showing that Christianity grew in the most isolated of places. Local people felt the need to build and worship to the glory of God as a sign of their faithfulness.

The panels at the base of the C15 tower include a crowned 'M' monogram for dedication to Mary and the IHS monogram for Jesus Christ. They are thought to be the work of the Aldryche family of North Lopham, Norfolk.

Also featured are the names of the local people who paid for the tower, among them Alice Skeet who left 20 sheep (10 wethers, 10 ewes) 'towards the buying of the bells'.

Today there is just one bell cast by Robert Gurney of Bury St Edmunds in 1663.

Discover more...

- The carved panel of an animal over the Norman south door. Is it a lion as author Pevsner suggests? Is it the Paschal lamb, or is it a wolf symbolising destruction? You decide

- The round-headed priest's door in the chancel, curiously moved from the north to the south side, leaving one half of a window now filled with 1950s glass depicting St Francis among Breckland flora and fauna

- Glass figures of Faith Hope and Charity by Victorian designer Charles Kempe. Faith is depicted in the narrow slit window in the nave and in the chancel you'll find Hope with her anchor, and Charity as Virgin Mary and child

- Remains of C13 foliage wall painting high up on the south wall of the nave

THE CLEANER'S WINDOW

C20 memorial window at Mildenhall St Mary IP28 7EE

Hidden away in the west end of this vast and beautiful building is a Victorian window dedicated to the church cleaner, Mary Anne Jolly. She diligently cleaned this magnificent medieval church for 18 years and died at the age of 89 in 1908.

Little else is known about her but this window, at the base of the tower, is a fitting tribute to the hundreds of volunteers down the centuries who quietly and regularly clean and care for our Suffolk churches.

The glass is by John Dudley Forsyth, apprentice to the renowned artist Henry Holiday. Forsyth's work also appears in Westminster Abbey, the Baltic Exchange London and Culford Church, Suffolk.

On the opposite side, the glass is dedicated to another woman, Mary Louisa Fordham, who rang the bells at St Mary's for 22 years and died in 1949.

Discover more...

- The mighty 120-foot tower completed in 1464
- The impressive vaulted ceilings in the two-storey north porch — largest in Suffolk — and under the west end gallery
- The breathtaking roof full of angels with outstretched wings. Spot the pike head embedded in one – thought to be the work of C17 Puritans
- The spectacular east window with its wonderful stone tracery dating back more than 600 years
- The beautifully carved 1950s bench ends made by an Ipswich craftsman and bequeathed to the church by architect Munro Cautley and his wife

In Memory of Mary Anne Jolly who for 18 years was a diligent cleaner of this church.

3

AN EXQUISITE WAGON ROOF

Early C16 wagon roof at Gazeley All Saints CB8 8RB

The early C16 wagon roof in the chancel is said to be the best of its kind in Suffolk. Wagon shaped and beautifully panelled, it features carved bosses of little angels bearing scrolls, wheat ears and vine leaves, as well as human faces.

Some of the original colour survives and the medieval glory of the roof, resplendent in vibrant colour, can only be imagined.

The nave roof, with its C16 tie-beams, has probably been lowered, judging from the sanctus bell window in the tower which is now above the roof line. Fortunately, the canted roof of the chancel was left alone, allowing us to marvel at the skills of those amazing medieval craftsmen.

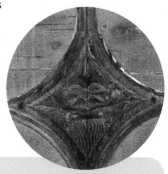

Discover more...

- C14 east window with, unusually, no containing arch at its apex
- The mystery of the arched recess in the south side of the sanctuary. Was it built as an aumbry for storing holy oil or as a very rare purpose-built recess for a small Easter sepulchre used symbolically over Good Friday and Easter to portray the burial and resurrection of Jesus?
- A tiny chalice brass near the sanctuary steps, one of only two surviving in Suffolk, commemorating a former parish priest who died about 1530
- Beautifully carved piscina, a stone basin for draining water used in the Mass, and the seating alongside for the priests known as sedilia, installed when the present chancel was built in the early 1300s

A TRUE SUFFOLK SAINT

St Edmund statue at the Cathedral church of St James and St Edmund IP33 1LS

The bronze statue of St Edmund by Suffolk-born Dame Elisabeth Frink RA (1930-93) was commissioned in 1974 by West Suffolk County Council to commemorate the end of 970 years of independent administration. Completed in 1976, the statue is based on brasses of C12 crusaders and now stands on the lawn by the Norman tower.

The church of St James was founded by Abbott Anselm and part of the great abbey founded by King Canute in the C11 to house the remains of the martyred King Edmund, killed by the Danes in 869. A new Gothic revival tower, a legacy of the architect Stephen Dykes Bower, was added to mark the millennium.

The cathedral added the dedication of St Edmund to its title in 2009 and there are numerous references to the saint, in stained glass, statues, paintings and needlework.

Discover more...

- The magnificent Norman tower, built in the mid 12C by Abbott Anselm as the main entrance to the abbey. It has served as a bell tower since the Middle Ages
- The Treasury in the crypt displaying historic church silver plate from various parishes
- Painted and gilded vaulted tower ceiling completed in 2010
- The Bishop's throne or cathedra with its carvings of the wolves guarding the head of St Edmund. The throne, also known as the episcopal see, is placed in the Bishop's principal church and a symbol of the Bishop's authority. 'See' is also used to describe his area of authority which is the diocese
- An impressive collection of embroidered kneelers created in the 1960s and based on the blue woollen cloth of the Middle Ages. They depict each parish in the diocese. Can you find your village among them?

5

TOMB OF MARY TUDOR

C16 tomb at Bury St Edmunds St Mary IP33 1RT

The tomb is plain and simple but the magnificence of this parish church – one of the largest in England – is fitting for the resting place of Mary 'Rose' Tudor, Queen of France and Duchess of Suffolk.

Mary was the favourite sister of Henry VIII, whose break with Rome in the C16, led to the great changes known as the Reformation and the formation of what we now know as the Church of England.

Mary became Queen of France after her marriage to Louis XII and on his death, married Charles Brandon, Duke of Suffolk. She died in 1533 and was buried in the Abbey at Bury St Edmunds. When in 1539 the Abbey was dissolved during the Reformation, her body was transferred to St Mary's.

In 1784 her tomb was dismantled and her lead coffin opened. Locks of her long golden hair were cut off and one can be seen at Moyses Hall Museum in Bury St Edmunds. She was reburied and her original tomb top placed over her grave.

Discover more...

- Magnificent C15 roof featuring angels, saints, martyrs, prophets and kings
- The chantry chapel of C15 clothier John Baret with the exquisite roof above his tomb
- Glass above the chancel arch depicting the martyrdom of St Edmund and based on a design of a medieval pilgrim's badge
- Vast west window, paid for by local landowners as a thanksgiving for the bumper harvest of 1854

STATIONS OF THE CROSS

C21 Stations of the Cross at Bury St Edmunds St John IP33 1SN

Iain McKillop's dramatic and moving Stations of the Cross were dedicated in 2008. They were commissioned after a competitive challenge to the artists of the day and developed through interaction with members of the parish and a local school.

The Stations portray the physical pain and suffering of Christ as he struggled to the Cross and culminate in a station of the Risen Christ in the Lady Chapel. Today's worshippers follow His journey by moving around the church to each station.

This Victorian Gothic church was built in 1841, using local Woolpit brick, by architect William Ranger. The remodelling of the east end by John Drayton Wyatt 35 years later inspires people to look to heaven, the eyes being led upward by six tall candles on the altar towards the starry sky in the roof above.

Discover more...

- The soaring spire rising 160 ft into the sky that has been likened to 'Thunderbird One' from the TV series
- The colossal western arch with a glass screen allowing a view of the 1903 Good Shepherd window
- The crucifix over the pulpit from Oberammergau, Bavaria, the site of the famous passion play

7

AN ANCIENT CHANCEL

C13 chancel at Great Barton Holy Innocents IP31 2QS

The chancel was always the first part of the church to be built and remained the holiest part of the building. The one at Great Barton is one of the earliest in the diocese.

The word chancel comes from the Latin cancellus which means screen. The chancel is therefore the screened off part of the church. The Reformation broke down the barriers between priest and people with the destruction of the rood screen and rood loft.

This is a very spacious chancel with a C13 piscina, a stone basin for draining water used in the Mass, and sedilia (stone seats) for the priest and his assistants.

In the chancel is the memorial to Lt Gen Sir Henry Edward Bunbury who died in 1860. He was given the job of informing the captured Napoleon that he was to be exiled to St Helena after the Battle of Waterloo in 1815.

Discover more...

- Glass in the south aisle commemorates the Golden Jubilee of Queen Victoria in 1887 by Heaton, Butler and Bayne, curiously with the supporting figures of the Queen of Sheba and Queen Esther
- The carved dog on the bench end, in honour of the sheepdogs that were highly valued when wool was a key commodity of Suffolk and shepherds were encouraged to bring their dogs into church rather than leave them outside

HEADSTONE OF A ROYAL FALCONER

C17 headstone at Great Livermere St Peter IP31 1JR

Headstones in churchyards are full of intrigue and tell us much about our ancestors. An ancient stone at Great Livermere, just to the right as you enter the porch, has royal connections and marks the grave of the 'forkner' or falconer to three Stuart kings.

William Sakings, who died in 1689, was falconer to Charles I and survived Oliver Cromwell's Commonwealth to similarly serve Charles II and James II.

The job of the falconer was highly responsible and required contact with the birds on a daily basis, feeding them on a balanced diet and maintaining all their accessories. A falcon in full dive can travel at over 200 miles an hour and is probably the fastest bird in the sky.

A record of money warrants from October 1683 records that Sakings was paid £25 1s 10 3/4d for half a year, making him wealthy enough to afford a headstone.

Also in the churchyard are the graves of Margaret, his wife, and Edmund, their son, who died in 1682 aged 17.

Discover more...

- Consecration crosses in the nave that the Bishop would have anointed with holy oil in order to dedicate the church to God
- C14 wall painting opposite the main door thought to be part of a Three Living and Three Dead sequence, common as a *memento mori* in medieval art — a reminder of the inevitability of death
- Three decker pulpit – top level for sermons, middle level for bible readings and the lower level for the parish clerk
- Monument to Montague Rhodes James, best known today as establishing the genre of ghost stories

9

WINDOW FOR THE LAST SQUIRE

C20 stained glass at Flempton St Catherine IP28 6EL

SAINT JOHN the EVANGELIST

This window is placed here
in memory of
Sir John Wood DL JP a Baronet

The C20 window in the south wall commemorates Sir John Wood, last of the Hengrave squires and MP for Stalybridge, Greater Manchester, who died in 1951 at the age of 93.

It is by Gerald Edward Roberts Smith and features St Francis, St John the Evangelist and St Christopher against clear glass.

Gerald Smith (1883-1959) was an early member of the British Society of Master Glass Painters. In 1906 he joined the studio of master glass painter Archibald Keightley Nicholson and their work appears in several churches including the east window at Manchester Cathedral.

After Nicholson's death in 1937, Smith took over and replaced much glass in bombed city churches after WWII.

Pictured here is a detail of the Flempton window showing St John the Evangelist.

Discover more...

- Fine C14 double piscina, a stone basin in the sanctuary for draining the water used in the Mass

- Victorian bench ends with delicate leaf carvings, designed in 1885 by James Fowler of Louth

- 1890s glass by Clayton & Bell in the east window showing the Crucifixion. Their studio was one of the largest of the Victorian era and they were noted for their consistency in the use of colour

- George III Royal Arms dated 1763 is signed by the artist from Bury St Edmunds

THE RESOURCEFUL EARLY MASONS

C12 round tower at Little Saxham St Nicholas IP29 5LH

The base of this tower is thought to date right back to the Anglo Saxons, but it is the Norman craftsmanship that is outstanding and the tower still retains its early C12 Norman belfry, unlike so many round towers in Suffolk that were rebuilt.

Most of England's round tower churches are found in Suffolk and Norfolk where stone for corners was scarce and costly and they had to make do with local flint.

Inside, the tower arch is tall and narrow, of Saxon shape but possibly by Norman builders; above it is an opening, maybe for the sanctus bell ringer, or possibly as a place of refuge for goods and maybe even people if needed.

Discover more...

- The curious blind arch in the west wall, south of the tower arch. Is it a tomb recess, the old north door, or a lost chapel? No-one knows for sure
- The two pre-Reformation bells cast by the Brasyer family of Norwich in the C15 with their trademark shield depicting three bells and coronet
- Medieval benches displaying birds and beasts, including a walrus!
- A C17 bier for carrying a coffin or shrouded corpse
- Elegant curved C18 communion rails, rescued from the abandoned church at Little Livermere

11

A DEVOTIONAL CHANCEL

C20 re-ordering of the chancel at Chevington All Saints IP29 5QH

The creation of space and light around a west-facing altar, enabling the priest to face the congregation, has transformed this chancel into an area that lends itself to prayerful and meditative worship after the style of the Taizé ecumenical monastic order in France.

During the 1983-4 re-ordering of the chancel, the floor stones were re-shaped to provide the edge of a horse-shoe communion platform. The black tabernacle, where the reserved sacrament is held, now echoes the style of the altar.

The atmosphere works particularly well at the Eucharist when communicants receive the sacrament while standing round the altar.

With the C15 benches around the chancel, the whole feeling is one of holiness and Christian witness down the ages and facilitates a devotional form of worship.

Discover more...

- The Norman zigzag moulding over the south door arch
- Norman lancet, the single slit window in north wall
- Sealed C13 stone coffin by the pulpit, shown to contain the skeleton of a young priest whose hands were found on his breast. The remains of a leaden chalice had fallen from his hands and lay near his right shoulder
- Carved C14 chest featuring monkeys, birds and a dragon
- C15 bench end depicting a bagpipe player. This is one of a series of musicians, including a lute player and a trumpeter

CURIOUS HEADS ON THE BENCH ENDS

C15 oak pews at Hawkedon St Mary Magdalene IP29 4NN

Look closely at these amazing bench ends and you'll discover a diverse range of human heads including three moustachioed oriental monks under conical hats carved by C15 craftsmen and a woman with three ears of corn.

Medieval bench-ends often terminate (as here) in three-lobed poppyheads - derived from the French poupee, meaning a puppet or doll and sometimes applied to ships' figureheads, but also providing a very fitting symbol of the Holy Trinity.

St Mary's stands in the middle of a green in the village centre and this sense of close community is echoed within the church itself.

Discover more...

- C12 square Norman font with carved panels
- 1708 heraldic hatchment over the entrance with unusual crossed bones and skull
- Royal Arms painted for Charles II later amended for George II by painting G for C and dating it 1750, with Queen Anne's motto added and removed in between
- Jacobean pulpit with small panels under the rim
- Medieval glass reset in the east window, including C17 continental saints in the upper lights, one of whom is St James with his pilgrim's staff

13

BEASTS ON THE BENCH ENDS

C15 benches at Denston St Nicholas CB8 8PP

The woodworker's art is superbly displayed in this church, most notably in the low C15 benches that stand on sills designed to keep straw or rushes in place to keep feet warm.

Over 50 carvings of fantastic creatures adorn the tops and armrests of the bench ends, including a unicorn, cockatrice, and a strange elephant with fan-shaped ears and a long nose.

Real or mythical, all had a place in the medieval bestiary, created in the belief that the natural world had been designed by God to instruct mankind on how to behave. Whether or not people believed the creatures actually existed, they served as a visual language for the illiterate.

Discover more...

- Seven sacrament font, said to be the only one in East Anglia made from the oatmeal-coloured stone that author Munro Cautley believed came from Aubigny in Normandy
- The macabre, shrouded effigies in the chancel quite possibly representing John Denston and his wife Katharine. It was under Denston's will that a chantry 'college' was founded in 1475 – an association of 'chantry priests' who could be employed to say prayers for those wealthy enough to pay
- Brass to Henry Everard and his wife Margaret in full Tudor regalia
- The many memorials to the Robinsons who took over the manor of Denston in 1617, including the restored C15 heraldic tabard hanging in the south chapel
- The misericords in the chancel, one depicting a crane with a stone in its claw. A misericord is a small carved shelf to the underside of the choir stall used as a 'mercy seat' to take the weight off the legs when the seat itself is tipped up

THE BARNARDISTON MONUMENTS

Early C17 monument at Kedington St Peter and St Paul CB9 7NN

14

One of the most striking of over 20 monuments to the Barnardiston family over more than 27 generations, is the figure of Grisell Barnardiston dated 1609.

Raised up on the south wall to the east of this wonderful church she is resplendent in Elizabethan costume with her hair ornately mounted on a high frame, as was the tradition in the early C17.

Baptised at Tottenham in 1593, Grisell died unmarried at the age of 16 and the rather poignant inscription tells us she was 'too wise, too choice, too old in youthful breath. 'Too deare to Frendes, too much of men desir'd. Therefore bereaft us with untymely death.'

The church is unusually rich in monuments and long referred to as the Westminster Abbey of Suffolk. Most of the memorials commemorate members of the Barnardiston family who were Lords of the Manor of Kedington from the C13 until 1745. They settled at the time of the Norman conquest and took their name from the village of Barnardiston, two miles to the north of Kedington.

Discover more...

- In the chancel is a Saxon cross that may well date back to the early C10 when it might have formed the head of an outdoor preaching cross. It depicts Christ, crucified but reigning in glory and victory over death
- Family box pews from the 1600s to the 1800s, one with its own fireplace!
- The elaborately carved manorial pew built by the Barnardistons in 1610
- Triple decker Jacobean pulpit with sounding board, wig stand and hour glass. One of the country's finest, it was used by the Puritan vicar Samuel Fairclough who preached at the Bury St Edmunds witch trials. His successor, John Tillotson, became Archbishop of Canterbury in 1691

15

BEER FOR THE RINGERS

C18 ringers' gotch at Clare St Peter and St Paul CO10 8PB

The gotch is a beer jug presented to the bell ringers by the vicar in 1729. It is made of semi-glazed earthenware for 32 pints and inscribed 'Clare Ringers 1729' and 'campana sonant canore' which translates as 'the bells ring in harmony'.

Over the centuries church bells were, and still are, an audible reminder to people that a service was about to begin and that they should make their way to church.

The vicar - aptly named the Revd Matthew Bell - happened to own the inn, the Six Bells, located at the north-west corner of the present graveyard.

Mr Bell's family also owned the Crown Inn which explains the embossed crown as well as the bell on the gotch.

Discover more...

- C15 eagle lectern with unusual feet of dogs instead of lions. Coins placed in the slot in the beak would be taken out through the slot in the tail
- The Jacobean gallery pew in the south aisle thought to have been built by Sir Thomas Barnardiston, owner of Clare Priory and sometimes known as the Priory Pew. Venture up and admire the view from the top of the stairs
- The sun and the moon in the east window, an example of the exquisite glass that must have filled the window before the Puritan William Dowsing wreaked destruction in the church
- The C18 sundial over the porch that says: 'Go about your business'. The porch was more than just an entrance in those days with all sorts of business transacted there

AN EARLY WINEGLASS PULPIT

C15 pulpit at Stoke by Clare St John the Baptist CO10 8JA

Made in 1498 this pulpit is one of the smallest in England – a mere 20 inches wide inside. It is one of just over 100 pre Reformation wooden pulpits remaining in England and is of the typical wineglass shape of the period with elaborate tracery.

The earliest pulpits date from around 1340 and may well have been erected because of popularity of itinerant preachers in the C14, notably the Franciscan friars.

Otherwise, people attended church mainly to celebrate the Mass and would see only the back of the priest as he stood at the altar beyond the rood screen.

This church was part of a Benedictine priory before becoming a college of priests – Stoke College — of which Matthew Parker was the last Dean, appointed by Anne Boleyn, as her favourite chaplain. He was also guardian of Elizabeth I who made him Archbishop of Canterbury.

Discover more...

- Fragments of medieval glass in the side chapel. Note the hart and the post mill, but particularly the roundel containing the arms of the Clothworkers Company showing the teazle used to raise the nap of the cloth and two tenterhooks used to fasten the cloth on to a tenter or drying frame. The cloth industry dominated medieval Suffolk

- Doom wall painting by the organ, depicting Christ seated on a rainbow and thought to have been painted during the C16 Catholic revival of Mary I's reign

- Outside on the north side, a one-handed clock with diamond-shaped dial, whose bell may have been cast in 1510 by an itinerant founder who inscribed the words: Surge mane servire Deo or 'Rise in the morning to serve God'

17

A FLEMISH MASTERPIECE

C16 reredos at Cavendish St Mary CO10 8AZ

As you enter the south door of Cavendish church, your eye will be immediately drawn by the sumptuous C16 Flemish altarpiece, lavishly gilded and coloured in alabaster.

A three dimensional relief, it depicts the three crosses of Calvary rising above a crowd of animated figures. It is no longer behind the altar but hung on the north wall and set in an elaborate frame by the distinguished architect Sir Ninian Comper (1864-1960).

The reredos came from the private chapel of the London home of the prominent Anglo Catholic layman Athelstan Riley who was one of the compilers of the English Hymnal. It was presented to St Mary's in 1953 by Riley's daughter Morwenna Brocklebank.

Discover more...

- C14 tower with handsome octagonal stair turret rising above the battlements
- Chancel dated to 1381, with $40 bequeathed by Sir John Cavendish, chief justice of the King's Bench in the reign of Richard II who was beheaded during the Peasants Revolt
- Fine C20 glass in the south aisle, one in memory of Emmeline Edmonds with Virgin and Child flanked by angels bearing shields with the Sacred Heart and St Edmund
- C21 plaque on south wall commemorating the lives and social work of Leonard Cheshire and Sue Ryder who established the Cheshire Homes and Sue Ryder Homes respectively. The couple are buried in the churchyard
- Rare and beautiful C15 eagle lectern and a C16 wooden reading desk for chained books

POLEY MONUMENTS

C17 monuments at Boxted Holy Trinity IP29 4LN

The magnificent alabaster monuments in the north chapel commemorate Sir John Poley (1558-1638) and his wife, Abigail. He served under Henry IV of France for three years and King Christian of Denmark for 22 years.

Boxted has been the seat of the Poley and Weller-Poley family for 600 years and you will see many monuments to these families in the chancel. In the north chapel, an open book and scroll trace the descent of the family from the C14 to the C20.

These grand monuments were erected half a century after the deaths of their subjects and Abigail's, dated 1725, is believed to be the last English monument made of alabaster. Sir John has a golden frog earring, the reason for which is unknown but one theory links it to the rhyme:

*'The frog he would a wooing go,
With a Roley Poley Gammon and Spinach'*

Why? Because among the local Boxted families were the Roleys, Poleys, Bacons and Greens.

Discover more...

- The C16 black effigies of William and Alice Poley in the chancel representing a rare revival of the wooden effigies seen in the C13
- Stuart pulpit with canopy to act as a sounding board dating from 1618
- C20 east window memorial to Hugh Thomas Weller-Poley killed at the age of 20 while serving in the RAF in 1942. The glass, by William Aikman, shows the figure of Christ in Glory with scenes from the Boxted parish underneath, including rabbits from the former warren

19

MYSTERY OF THE MAGI PANEL

C14 alabaster panel at Long Melford Holy Trinity CO10 9DT

The really intriguing thing about this panel depicting the Adoration of the Magi is that it dates from about 1350 and is 130 years older than the present magnificent church. Dug up from under the chancel floor in the C18, it may have formed part of an alabaster altar hidden during the Reformation in the hope that it would one day be discovered.

The Magi are described in St Matthew's Gospel as 'wise men from the East' and were widely regarded as being able to read the stars. They were the first non-Jewish people to show devotion to the newly-born Christ child and presented him with gifts of gold, frankincense and myrrh.

Discover more...

- One of the finest collections of medieval glass in the country in the north aisle. The roundel of three hares over the north door has each of the ears shared by two hares so that only three ears are shown. In Christian churches, this is a symbol of the Holy Trinity – God, Jesus the Son and the Holy Spirit
- The Lily Crucifix window in the beautiful Clopton Chantry chapel, the lily symbolising the suffering shared by the Virgin Mary and her son Jesus
- The separate Lady Chapel built around 1496 with multiplication table dating from 1670 when the Chapel was first used as a village school

REMARKABLE GILDED FONT COVER

C15 font cover at Sudbury St Gregory CO10 1AZ

The great treasure of this church is the spectacular font cover made in about 1450 when a major part of the building was constructed. Its soaring 12ft height and rich gilding reflect the importance of baptising new members into the family of the Church.

It is not known when the cover was made telescopic to enable the lower octagonal drum to be raised, leaving the triple tier of tracery in place.

The cover has been restored to show how the original colouring would have looked and it is thought that the niches contained the figures of saints when the cover was made.

Discover more...

- Early C16 chancel ceiling restored to its original colours in 1966
- Late C20 Stations of the Cross by Nicholas Mynheer
- The first misericord on the south side of the chancel bears the badge of Simon of Sudbury who founded a college of canons and extended the chancel for their use. He became Archbishop of Canterbury in 1375 and Chancellor in 1380 when he imposed  the poll tax and was subsequently beheaded during the Peasants' Revolt. You can ask to see his head, locked in the vestry, if the church is manned when you visit

GEM OF A WOODEN PORCH

C14 north porch at Boxford St Mary CO10 5DX

This church has two fine medieval porches, the C15 stone porch on the south side and the miraculously-preserved, timber-built north porch which is over 100 years older. Considered one of the best of its period, the porch features fine carving and panelling and the ceiling has an intriguing mixture of wooden joists and ribs. Experts claim it shows the way in which C14 carpenters copied the patterns and designs of the masons before developing their own.

Church records show that in 1820, the rector and churchwardens recommended it should be 'taken down' due to it being in such a bad state of repair so we are indeed fortunate to be able to see it today.

Discover more...

- C17 font cover opens out to reveal texts painted on red and cream scrolls
- Wall painting of St Edmund with his arrow in south aisle Lady chapel
- Monument to Elizabeth Hyam 'hastened to her end' due to a fall in 1748 in her 113th year
- Vibrant east window depicting the Transfiguration of Christ by Rosemary Rutherford and installed in 1973

THE PURITAN PIONEER

C19 east window for John Winthrop at Groton St Bartholomew CO10 5ED

Our treasure in this hilltop church is the brightly coloured east window dedicated to the memory of John Winthrop, one of America's founding fathers, and given by his American descendants.

Dating back to 1875, the window is by Cox & Sons and contains scenes showing Moses instructing the Hebrews to serve God faithfully so that 'he will bless you in the land which he is giving you', and the Apostle Paul imploring the elders of Ephesus to turn to God in repentance and have faith in Jesus.

Winthrop was Lord of the Manor at Groton in 1618, like his father before him, but used his wealth to organise a fleet of 11 ships to lead a wave of Puritan immigrants to New England in 1630.

He had mourned the decline of the 'godly kingdom of the Stour Valley' under the reign of Charles I but eventually became first governor of the Massachusetts Bay Colony and founder of the city of Boston.

Groton Suffolk treasures its links with the town of Groton Massachusetts.

Discover more...

- The table tomb between south aisle and chancel, the grave of John Winthrop's parents Adam and Anne and his grandfather, also Adam
- Glass in the south aisle where many members of the Winthrop family are commemorated
- What is believed to be the oldest gravestone in Suffolk dated 1598 to the memory of 'Lewes Kedbye whoe had to wife Jane Kedbye'. His family was later connected by marriage to the Winthrops

23

WALL PAINTINGS REVEALED

Early wall paintings at Brent Eleigh St Mary CO10 9NP

When the east wall needed repairing in 1961 and traces of colour were seen, no-one realised that a closer inspection would reveal some of the finest wall paintings in England, dating between 1270 and 1330.

The three paintings portray the crucified Christ flanked by the Virgin Mary below the east window with St John with censing angels (offering incense) to the left of it, and the remains of the Harrowing of Hell to the right.

The latter probably dates from the early C13 and is thought to be extremely rare. The Harrowing of Hell depicts the triumphant descent of Christ into Hell or Hades between the time of his crucifixion and his resurrection, to bring salvation to the souls there. This painting is very faint but it is just possible to see him rescuing Adam from the 'pit' of hell.

Discover more ...

- Early C14 south door with lovely carving and original ironwork
- C13 octagonal Purbeck marble font with Jacobean font cover
- Rare example of a coloured C14 screen to the south east chapel
- Georgian three-sided communion rails of which there are only a few in East Anglia
- Dramatic memorial in the chancel to Edward Colman, who died in the 1740s. His father bequeathed a library of over 1,000 books to the church, now dispersed
- Kneelers worked by parishioners and friends with designs from tiles and carvings in the church

SEATS THAT TELL A TALE

C14 misericords at Lavenham St Peter & St Paul CO10 9RZ

Misericords are the hinged wooden seats that tip up to reveal a small shelf that provides support for the user during lengthy prayers without actually sitting down.

In medieval Latin, misericordia means mercy and these did indeed provide 'mercy seats' to lean upon.

In Lavenham the wonderful collection of misericords represents one of the many outstanding features in this magnificent and nationally-important church.

In St Peter and St Paul, the intriguing carvings on the misericords include a man and woman, half-human, half-beast, he playing a fiddle with a pair of tongs, she a hurdy-gurdy, as well as the more familiar medieval image of the pelican in her piety, plucking at her breast to feed her young with her own blood.

Discover more ...

- The landmark tower, over 140 ft high, begun in 1486 at the behest of the Lord of the Manor John de Vere, Earl of Oxford

- Elaborately carved Spring Parclose or chapel of 1525 with the tombs of the church's benefactor, the wealthy clothier Thomas Spring and his wife, Alice. Note the images on its corners of Catherine of Alexandria and Bishop Blaise, patron saint of wool combers

- Huge range of colourful Victorian picture windows throughout the church

- The exquisitely worked choir stall ends crafted by C19 carver Henry Ringham of Ipswich

EARLY FONT REFLECTS NORMAN ORIGINS

C12 font at Kettlebaston St Mary IP7 7QA

Village infants have been baptised in this ancient font for over 800 years. Rare in Suffolk, though with a 'twin' in neighbouring Preston, this Norman font dates back to around 1180 and has a square bowl with original supports.

During the first 100 years of Norman rule, thousands of churches were built of stone for the first time. Stars, chevrons and dog's tooth markings were distinctively Norman and appear on this font, the latter also round the south doorway. Could this indicate it was the work of the same mason?

This church reflects the styles of every century since the church was built around 1180. In the C19, it became a focus of the Anglo-Catholic tradition following the emergence of the Oxford Movement of which nearby Hadleigh was a focal point, and this is still echoed in the vibrant colours, statues and altars.

Discover more ...

- Casts of C14 alabaster panels showing the Annunciation, Ascension, Trinity and Coronation of the Blessed Virgin Mary. The originals were found in 1864 and are now in the British Museum
- The slit or lancet window in the north wall, discovered in 1930, where the Norman 'dog tooth' motifs re-appear
- One of Suffolk's finest modern rood screens, designed by Father Ernest Geldart in 1890 and richly decorated in the C20
- At the time of writing, one of the last churches in regular use to depend on paraffin lamps for evening light

A CLASSIC FLUSHWORK PORCH

C16 flint flushwork porch at Preston St Mary CO10 9NQ

The glint of the fine flushwork of split flint, beautifully worked in panels and dressed with stone, draws you to this large and impressive north porch.

The elegant Grade I listed church is partly concealed behind a splendid yew tree reputed to have been planted at least 250 years before the porch was added. When a thunderbolt struck the tower for the second time in 1868 causing major destruction, both porch and tree remained intact.

The flushwork covers the sides of the porch as well as the front, there are niches and battlements, and over the door are the emblems of the Passion and the Trinity contained in two shields.

Inside, the small door to the church is offset to leave space for the altar tomb, thought to be that of the porch builder.

The church porch not only gave shelter, but had several uses; mothers were 'churched' here to thank God for the safe birth of a child, wedding vows exchanged, Baptism services began, charity distributed, and business transacted.

Discover more ...

- A triptych bearing the Ten Commandments or 'Decalogue' is visible when not loaned out to for national exhibition This decalogue board could well date back to Edward VI who stringently enforced Protestant reforms
- The Royal Arms of Elizabeth I, also in oak in the form of a triptych, were painted on the orders of Robert Ryece of Preston Hall who died in 1638. It is believed he had the original board – bearing the arms of Edward VI — cut down to match the decalogue boards
- C12 Norman font with rosettes, stars, intersected arches, and a tree of life mounted on 19C stonework
- C17 glass with 52 heraldic shields in the nave and clerestory windows, just a third of those collected by Robert Ryece of Preston Hall, a student of heraldry

THE RARE SACRING BELL

C15 sacring bell at Hawstead All Saints IP29 5NT

A rare survival is fixed to the late C15 chancel screen. It is the wooden 'stirrup' for a sacring bell and remarkably still contains what is thought to be the original bell.

The sacring bell served the same purpose for the people inside the church as the sanctus bell did for those outside. It was rung to proclaim the climax of the Mass. It sounded therefore at the Sanctus ('Holy, holy, holy…'), just before the consecration of the bread and wine, then when the newly consecrated bread was held up for the people to see, then likewise the wine.

The south-west chancel window incorporates a low-side opening, which once had a shutter which opened to allow a sanctus bell to be rung at the same time so that people in the neighbourhood who could not be present could pause and join in prayer.

Discover more ...

- The monument to Elizabeth Drury who died in 1609 aged 14 with the result that the famous English poet John Donne sent her grieving parents verses that later became known as 'A Funerall Elegie'. It is one of some 40 monuments in the church, many to the powerful Drury family
- Late C13 effigy of cross-legged knight said to be Sir Eustace Fitz-Eustace, one of the early Lords of the Manor of Hawstead who died in 1271 and the earliest monument in the church
- The roundel in the centre window of the north aisle depicting the wolf finding the head of St Edmund, a C20 copy of the original in the Cathedral
- Fine glass by Victorian glass artist Henry Holiday in the south aisle, one depicting Archangels Gabriel, Michael and Raphael

THE SEVEN DEADLY SINS

C14 wall painting at Hessett St Ethelbert IP30 9AX

Hessett is famous for its wall paintings that provided a visual aid to medieval churchgoers, many of whom were not literate and could not understand the Latin of the scriptures and services. There is no mistaking the message of the Seven Deadly Sins - pride, lust, sloth, avarice, anger, envy and gluttony - portrayed as figures on the branches of a tree springing from the jaws of hell with demons on either side.

The painting, on the north wall, dates from 1370 and is thought to be the fullest and clearest depiction of this theme in the country.

Immediately below is a rare representation of Christ of the Trades, dating from about 1430. Christ is surrounded by pincers, hammer, scissors, chisel and gridiron, the message being a warning to would-be Sabbath breakers not to use such tools on a Sunday.

Discover more ...

- Medieval iron-bound chest which saved from Cromwell's men a very rare burse used for carrying the corporal (part of the altar linen), and an equally rare pyx cloth to veil the receptacle that holds the sacrament above the altar. These are now in the British Museum but are pictured in the church
- Lots of gorgeous medieval glass even though many of the heads were replaced in the C19
- Royal Arms of Charles II, apparently modified for the reign of Queen Anne but since altered back to their original design
- What remains of the C15 rood screen

A ROOF FULL OF SAINTS AND ANGELS

C15 double hammer beam roof at Woolpit St Mary IP30 9QG

Look up when you enter this beautiful church to see the great glory of the building, the mid-C15 double hammerbeam roof full of saints, angels, bishops and kings.

Some of the figures are original; others by Suffolk's master woodworker Henry Ringham of Ipswich in 1844. The angels he carved replaced those destroyed in 1644 during Cromwell's Commonwealth and this was his first important commission.

Woolpit was a wealthy parish in medieval times, being popular with pilgrims visiting the chapel of Our Lady of Woolpit and the Lady's Well, which reputedly had healing powers for eye afflictions.

Discover more ...

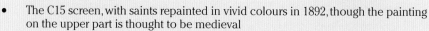

- The splendid C15 porch, thought to be one of the best of its kind in the country. Could it really have taken 40 years to build?
- The remarkable range of animal carvings on the bench ends including dogs, griffins and a chained monkey. Some are C15 and likely to have been the work of local craftsmen; the front rows are by Henry Ringham
- The C15 screen, with saints repainted in vivid colours in 1892, though the painting on the upper part is thought to be medieval
- C16 lectern supposedly gifted to the church by Queen Elizabeth I on her visit
- Victorian glass in the tower's west window made in 1848 by Lucy Marriott, the wife of the curate at Onehouse – one of two women glass painters in Suffolk at that time

ST EDMUND ON THE WALL

Ancient wall paintings at Troston St Mary IP31 1EX

These wall paintings are centuries old and some of the finest and most important in East Anglia.

The smaller painting of St George could well date back to the mid C13. The large paintings of St Christopher with the infant Christ on his shoulder and St George slaying the dragon are dated 1380/1400. There is also a further C14 painting - a rare depiction of the martyrdom of St Edmund which shows the king shot with the arrows of four archers.

The paintings were recently cleaned and stabilised by conservator Andrea Kirkham.

Over the chancel arch is a fragment of a late C15 Doom painting. The figure of Christ seated in judgement is in the centre.

Discover more ...

- One of the best sets of medieval graffiti in Suffolk. Good examples on the chancel arch and on the south side of the tower arch
- Four consecration crosses to find on the walls marking the places the Bishop annointed with holy oil when he reconsecrated the rebuilt nave in the C14
- C17 pulpit to which an oversized reading desk has been added
- Glass in the east window by Harry Stammers, 1964, one of his finest, showing Christ in the centre with a disciple on either side

31

THE BARDWELL GLASS

C15 stained glass at Bardwell St Peter & St Paul IP31 1AH

This C15 glass panel is one of the earliest and most complete in Suffolk. It is a portrait of Sir William Berdewell (1367-1434) who is thought to have built the tower, the hammerbeam nave roof and the south porch, the latter bearing his arms.

Berdewell, later Bardwell, was a professional soldier from his youth and entered the service of the Duke of Suffolk in 1400. Known as 'the great warrior', he was Henry V's standard bearer in the French wars and probably served at Agincourt.

Look closely to make out his gold-rimmed glasses!

Sir William and his wife, Margaret de Pakenham, are buried in the chancel.

Discover more...

- Magnificent hammerbeam roof where the weight is supported by 'hammer' brackets, resplendent with much of its original colour. The roof has been dated to 1421 from a book held by a remaining wooden figure
- South porch showing the fine craftsmanship of the C15. Note the tiny flowers just below the parapet
- Colourful modern kneelers depicting scenes of village life, worked in the 1970s
- Mighty 87ft tower visible for miles

KINGS IN THE ROOF

C16 clerestory at Hopton All Saints IP22 2QY

This early Tudor clerestory is distinctive in red brick and handsomely embattled. Inside, the clear light from seven pairs of windows emphasises the late medieval hammerbeam roof. The hammer beams themselves are actually ermine-collared figures of kings and musicians holding variously books, chalice and the patens typically used to hold the bread for the Eucharist. They were repainted by the vicar's five daughters in the late C19, work that could well have been inspired by the work of Mildred Holland at Huntingfield.

Discover more...

- The fine medieval door to the tower stairs at the back of the south aisle, with original interlaced ironwork and hinge, a reminder that church property and parish valuables were kept there for safety
- Marble tablet in the chancel in memory of Thomas Raymond who died in 1680 and was keeper of the state papers of Charles II
- The 1890s glass in the east window by Thomas Figgis Curtis of Ward & Hughes where the faces appear to be of real people

33

KALEIDOSCOPIC GLASS

C20 stained glass windows at Hinderclay St Mary IP22 1HN

The C20 glass that floods this church with coloured light is the work of East Anglian artist Rosemary Rutherford.

The Nativity, the Crucifixion and the Resurrection are featured in one of the windows in the south aisle and this is some of the best of Rutherford's work.

The glass in the east window represents the Tree of Life, the Transfiguration of Christ and the River of Life.

Born in Broomfield, Essex, the artist was the sister of the rector at nearby Walsham le Willows and later settled in Suffolk. She studied at the Slade in the 1930s and produced a body of work that depicted her experiences with the Red Cross in WW2, including driving a mobile canteen round defence batteries on the east coast.

Rosemary Rutherford died in 1972 at the age of just 60.

Discover more...

- Diamond-shaped poppyheads on the west end pews with rosettes and fleurs-de-lys dated 1617. The letters carved on them are thought to be the initials of churchwardens
- One of few wooden porches in this part of Suffolk with a C14 outer arch

GARLAND FOR A TRAGIC MAIDEN

C17 maiden's crant at Walsham le Willows St Mary IP31 3AB

The unusual wooden medallion in the nave records the death of Mary Boyce aged 20 in 1685. It is widely thought to be part of a maiden's garland, also known as a virgin's crant or crown, from the German krantz meaning a wreath. The disc is made of elm wood and below the name is a heart pierced by an arrow as it is said that, tragically, Mary died of a broken heart.

The ancient custom was to hang a garland in the church as a funerary memento for a chaste young woman cheated by death of her marriage. In earlier times the disc would have been hung with garlands annually.

The practice occurs in Shakespeare's Hamlet. Ophelia is denied the full funeral rites:'…yet here she is allow'd her virgin crants, her maiden strewments (strewn flowers)…'

Discover more...

- The lovely medieval oak roof, supported by alternating tie-beams and hammer-beams and featuring roses en soleil, said to be Edward IV's favourite badge with the original colouring clearly visible
- The chancel screen dated 1448 has original painted stencils but the carved wooden surrounds were painted in 1842
- The altar reredos, by national terracotta artist George Tinworth 1883, is a depiction of the Last Supper of Jesus and his disciples
- Memorial window featuring St Dorothy in the chancel to Rosemary Rutherford, stained glass artist and sister of the rector, who died in 1972
- Huge pinnacles depicting the armorial beasts of Edward IV at the top of the tower, hauled up around 1475

35

WILD FLOWERS IMMORTALISED IN GLASS

C15 wild flower window at Gislingham St Mary IP23 8HP

The lower sections of the three lights of the window east of the pulpit contain some of the earliest illustrations of English wild flowers, beautifully depicted in colourful C15 stained glass and forming intricately designed wreaths surrounding the coats of arms of the Toppesfield, Chirche (or Ashfield) and Clouting families.

The wreaths contain intertwined stems, with leaves and tendrils and the western and eastern panels have little blue flowers which have been identified as blue columbine.

The pairs of little white flowers in the central panel are a mystery.

Discover more …

- Magnificent double hammerbeam roof in the nave
- Handsome C15 font. Can you spot the arms of St Edmund on one of the panels?
- Set of 1810 box pews surrounding the three-decker pulpit of 1802
- The sturdy brick tower of 1638, replacing one which collapsed in 1599
- Record of a peal of bells on a board surrounded by the tools of the ringer's trade
- The kneeling figure in the chancel, white gloves in hand, of Lord of the Manor and London merchant, Anthony Bedingfield who died in 1652

MEMORIAL BY WWI SOLDIERS

1914-18 memorial shrine at Burgate St Mary IP22 1QE

Fresh from serving as an army chaplain, Benjamin Appleyard, who was rector at Burgate 1919-1940, set up this remarkable memorial shrine in a blocked arch in the chancel.

The woodwork of its low steps and altar is by Potter & Sons of Wortham.

The vessels and ornaments were made in 1917 by wounded soldiers at Godwaersvelde Hospital near Ypres from shell cases.

Beneath a central canopy are Appleyard's wartime communion vessels and nearby is his tin hat.

The text within the arch reads:

'Greater love hath no man than this, that a man lay dow his life for his friends'.

Discover more ...

- The faces of Harry Baker and Billy Garrod, Burgate choristers, bellringers and churchwardens, sculpted in stone by Terence Sandy in 1995, each side of the doorway as you enter
- The magnificent tomb with fine brasses of Sir William de Burgate who died in 1409 and his Lady wife Alianora, he with a lion at his feet and she with a dog
- Photograph of Benjamin Appleyard and other rectors in the St Edmund chapel at the north west end of the nave

37

A RICHLY PAINTED ROOF

Painted hammerbeam roof at Palgrave St Peter IP22 1AG

Whereas most of Suffolk's splendid hammerbeam roofs are many feet above you, Palgrave's nave roof is low enough to enjoy it at reasonably close quarters. And what beautiful and unusual C15 craftsmanship this is.

Most of the county's hammerbeam roofs are decorated with carvings, this one is painted – and exquisitely so. In fact, much of the original colouring has remained.

There is fine woodcarving in the cornices at the tops of the walls and decorating the hammer beams; also notice the sawn-off tenons where the angels once fitted.

Discover more ...

- St Michael and the dragon carved into the entrance arch of the south porch
- Late Norman font that has hosted over 800 years of Palgrave baptisms
- Commandment boards, once over the altar but now in the north aisle, beautifully restored in the 1960s
- Colourful stained glass in a nave window designed in 1995 by Surinder Warboys from nearby Mellis

A SOARING SUFFOLK TOWER

The west tower at Eye St Peter and St Paul IP23 7BD

Soaring over 100 feet into the sky, the mighty church tower at Eye has been described as 'the wonder of Suffolk'.

Out walking or cycling, it is an impressive landmark.

It was built around 1450 and the powerful buttresses and entire west face are covered with exquisite patterns in knapped or split flint known as flushwork, a technique seen at its best in this diocese.

This beautifully-proportioned tower, a masterpiece of medieval craftsmanship and design, can be seen for miles but the most dramatic view is from the Eye castle mound that provides one of the grandest views of any English parish church.

Discover more ...

- Dramatic and colourful rood loft and rood group designed by Sir Ninian Comper in the 1920s. The font cover and east window are also his work
- Glorious rood screen dated from about 1480, featuring 15 exquisitely painted saints veritable medieval 'Old Masters', that still adorn the church for which they were painted
- Lough Pendred's Shrine of Our Lady, dated 1973 and set in a C14 tomb recess

39

LOCAL JOINER'S WORK OF ART

C17 font cover by local craftsman at Mendlesham St Mary IP14 5SG

This elaborate font cover with its Renaissance imagery and seahorse brackets was made by a local man John Turner in 1630.

It rises in two stages, the lower supported on Tuscan columns and the upper with obelisks rising from it.

During the C19, it fell into disrepair and was removed to the clock chamber where it remained for about 50 years. It was restored and put back in 1908.

Turner, a skilled craftsman, also made the intricately carved pulpit.

Discover more ...

- The Lady Chapel altar table, over 400 years old, has one leg carved the wrong way round
- Look for the C15 bench end depicting a dragon biting his curled tail, commonly regarded as a symbol of infinity. Discover other intricate bench ends
- Crowned lions and wild men known as woodwoses armed with clubs adorning the parapet of the lavish porch
- The lion with his tongue out in 700-year-old glass from Southolt in the north aisle
- The brass of John Knyvet, near the nave altar. Note his beard, depicted outside his armour

PRICELESS MEDIEVAL PANEL

C14 altar retable at Thornham Parva St Mary IP23 8EY

The oak panel painting or retable behind the altar in this tiny church has miraculously survived over six and a half centuries and is now recognised as one of the greatest treasures of medieval art in Europe.

This retable and the Musée de Cluny frontal in Paris were part of a work that adorned the high altar in the Dominican Priory at Thetford and were probably produced in a workshop in or near the town for that very purpose.

The astonishing fact is that this piece of work lay forgotten for decades – bought by an ancestor of Lord Henniker of Thornham Magna at the sale of a farm in Stradbroke in 1778 and turning up in the stable loft of Thornham Hall in 1927 when the then Lord Henniker handed it over to the church.

A major restoration in 1998 dated the work to the 1330s and today you can clearly see the Crucifixion scene at the centre with St Dominic and St Catherine, left, balanced by St Margaret and St Peter Martyr at the other end, while St John the Baptist and St Peter (third and fourth from left) correspond to the opposite pair of St Paul and St Edmund.

Discover more ...

- Outstanding C14 wall paintings, including the north doorway arch which doubles as a bridge for St Edmund's cart
- In the churchyard, the grave of Sir Basil Spence, architect of Coventry Cathedral who died in 1976
- Glass by Laurence Whistler in the nave, one with a quotation from Shakespeare

FLINT FLUSHWORK AT ITS BEST

Gipping Chapel of St Nicholas IP14 4PT

Discover more ...

- Magnificent east window packed with mostly fragmented medieval glass
- The purpose built organ by Peter Bumstead 1994
- The chimney shaft in the north chapel, now the vestry, cleverly concealed from the outside and the inscription carved into the arch over the doorway: 'Pray for Sir Jamys Tirell. Dame Anne his Wye'

This beautiful building was built as a private chapel 1474-80 for Sir James Tyrell the then Lord of the Manor at Gipping Hall, now vanished.

The richly decorated chequerboard pattern of the walls in knapped (split) flint, septaria and limestone is widely regarded as the finest in Suffolk. Vast windows present a greenhouse effect and numerous emblems, initials and arms of the Tyrell family decorate the walls, doorways and buttresses. Sir James was beheaded in 1502, having supported the 3rd Duke of Suffolk, claimant to the throne of Henry VII, and allegedly admitting to the murder of the Princes in the Tower while being tortured.

Inside, the east wall is decorated with rare C18 trompe l'oeil mural complete with draped columns and a swag. St Nicholas never has been a parish church and, since 1743, it has been a chapel administered by trustees who appoint a chaplain.

PEEP INSIDE AN C18 PRAYER BOOK

1793 altar prayer book at Old Newton St Mary IP14 4PP

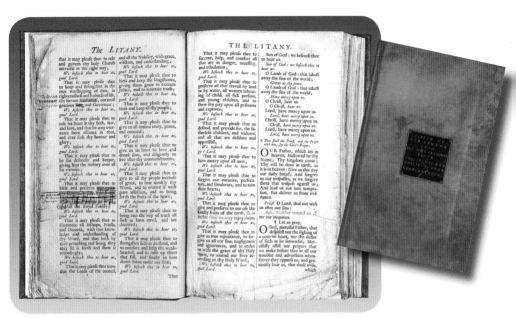

Discovered under the vestry floor during recent building work and now displayed in a glass case near the altar, this beautiful prayer book has been restored and rebound in calf skin. A cover plate dated 1800 gives the names of the then churchwardens and incumbent.

Different pages are displayed weekly but if you are lucky it may be open at the page showing how, in the interests of economy, the names of the Sovereign and other members of the Royal Family were amended.

Discover more ...

- C19 west gallery resting on slim cast iron pillars with seating for a large number and divided to keep the boys from the girls
- Fretwork war memorial on the north wall, carved by the brother of William Bowers Codd who died in 1917, aged 27. He is buried in the churchyard
- To fully appreciate the depth of the tower walls pop into the loo and look at the window!
- Walk round the outside of the church to compare elegant C14 windows in the nave with those in the chancel that were restored in the C19 when cast iron rather than brick or stone was used

43

THE GEORGIAN BARREL ORGAN

Working barrel organ at Shelland King Charles the Martyr IP14 3DE

This rare 1810 barrel organ plays 36 different tunes and is the only one left in the country in regular use.

Made by Henry Bryceson, London, who also built the first electric key-action organ which he installed in Drury Lane Theatre in 1862, this instrument is now a great curiosity.

The organ is activated by a person turning a crank. The pieces of music are encoded onto wooden barrels which correspond to the keyboard of the traditional pipe organ.

The Shelland organ features three original wooden barrels each containing 12 tunes. A new barrel was added in 2006 made by Bishop & Son of Ipswich and pinned by John Budgen from Wiltshire

Until 1936 the church was privately owned by, among others, Thomas Cropley, a fierce Royalist. He was imprisoned and died in 1659 and then his loyal family rededicated the church to King Charles the Martyr, making it one of only six so dedicated in England.

Discover more...

- The extraordinary C18 'Gothick' decor said by some to refer to the colours of the walls of the New Jerusalem in Revelation 21 v 19, and by others to the colours chosen by the local wainwright, because they matched his wagons, when he was ordered to paint the church
- The complete set of box pews with matching triple-decker pulpit with reading desk, clerk's pew and nearby hat pegs, dated 1767
- The C14 octagonal limestone font with its carved foliate patterns and shields, a reminder of the earlier, medieval building. The pineapple on the cover is a sign of wealth and welcome
- The altar rail with its close-packed balusters to prevent dogs getting inside the sanctuary

THE CREATURES IN THE ROOF

Exquisitely carved roof at Earl Stonham St Mary the Virgin IP14 5EE

Constructed in the C15 at a time when the best of everything was only just good enough for the church, this nave roof is a single hammerbeam with a span of 17 feet and six inches in 10 bays.

The carvings are numerous, detailed and quite beautiful. They show up the mutilation of William Dowsing in the 1640s, but careful inspection with binoculars will reveal an albatross, a fox with a goose in its mouth, an owl and a terrier. These together with hosts of angels and saints are powerful testimony to the determination of medieval craftsmen to remind us that all manner of creatures are there to worship God for whom this house of prayer has been created.

Discover more...

- The church is cross-shaped, the projecting 'arms' known as transepts. Note the complex and beautiful roofs of the transept and chancel
- Remains of medieval Doom painting of the 'Last Judgement' above the chancel arch and St George and the Dragon on the south transept wall
- C15 bench ends, including the man playing bagpipes in the choir stalls
- The nave pews, all the work of one local man James Gibbons, the carving done by Robert Godbold of Harleston, Norfolk in about 1874

AN AWE-INSPIRING ANGEL ROOF

Unique C15 roof at Needham Market St John the Baptist IP6 8DG

This spectacular development of a single hammerbeam roof represents medieval engineering at its best. Built in the second half of the C15 with no iron bolts, straps or nails, it was simply morticed and tenoned together and secured by wooden pegs. A thorough understanding of such techniques enabled those designers and craftsmen to construct awe-inspiring roofs which remain today to delight and inspire.

Records show that the roof was covered over for a period until 1880 when the plaster was removed. Today you can lie back on one of the choir stalls to relish the wonderful detail of this medieval masterpiece and marvel that there isn't another like it in England.

Discover more...

- Outside, the arch in the buttress so constructed to allow processions round the church to remain on consecrated ground because the site of church is limited
- Jack in the Green above the organ, dressed in a covering of green leaves a medieval pagan symbol of the tree spirit heralding the coming of summer
- Pilgrim figures in the porch dating from around the 16th century and representing St James of Compostela. Note the scallop-shell pilgrim's badge on one of them
- C20 Stations of the Cross – a set of paintings by Francis Hoyland depicting the last journey of Jesus

SONGS OF PRAISE

C18 musicians' gallery at Battisford St Mary IP14 2HF

The gallery at the west end of the church is as wide as the building and one of a few remaining that sprung up after many pipe organs were destroyed by Cromwell's Puritans and there was little to relieve the tedium of long services and sermons.

The West Gallery Music Association claims this tradition came out of a desire of parishioners around the late C17 to do more than sit in dull silence at the point where the psalm may be 'said or sung' and soon great hymn writers such as the Wesleys were inspiring village musicians all over the country.

The locals would lead the congregation and, at Battisford, Fred Mudd made stringed instruments using local wood and homemade tools. A wind instrument known as a serpent was also played here and is now housed in the museum at Christchurch Mansion in Ipswich.

Discover more...

- The font cover, presented to the church in 1967 to commemorate the presence of the Knights Hospitallers of the Order of St John of Jerusalem in the village. The knights held a half interest in the church in the C12

- The Royal Arms of Queen Anne, wrongly drawn. Find out why when you visit the church. Preceding Queen Anne, Queen Elizabeth I visited the church in the late C16

- Mary Everton's memorial in front of the altar step; she died aged 103 in 1608

RALPH'S HOLE

The hidden room at Hemingstone St Gregory IP6 9RF

This little room will transport you to the time in the C16 when all Roman Catholics were meant to transfer their allegiance to the Protestant faith. Ralph Cantrell did not want to worship as a Protestant but neither did he want problems with the authorities and this is his compromise.

He built this little room on the north side of the nave where he could sit comfortably, listen to the service through an opening called a squint but, for the sake of his conscience, not enter the church. The door to the chancel was added later.

Ralph was not the only problem to the authorities because it is recorded that in 1597 the entire parish was mentioned in the consistory court because they had not been attending regular worship as required by rules enacted in 1559.

Discover more...

- Splendid C14 font, elaborately carved
- William Cantrell's unusual tomb of 1585 with its interesting inscription
- C14 glass featuring sprays of foliage in the upper stone tracery of the window on the north side of the chancel, interesting because it is almost intact and 'in situ'

A RARE STONE SCREEN

C14 stone chancel screen at Bramford St Mary the Virgin IP8 4AT

Beneath the chancel arch and separating the nave from the chancel is the rare and beautiful stone screen. It is one of only about 50 in England as screens are commonly made of wood.

Screens were placed to mark the point beyond which members of the congregation could not go. Only priests were allowed into the chancel.

On top of the screen would have been the rood loft, above which was the great rood or cross with the crucified Christ flanked by his grieving mother Mary and his Apostle St. John. The positioning of the figures at this point in the church was a powerful reminder to the congregation of the focus of their worship.

There is only a small part of another stone screen remaining in a Suffolk church and that is at Little Wenham.

Discover more...

- Single hammerbeam roof constructed in about 1420
- The figure of St Edmund with his arrow outside the church on the north west corner of the porch
- Almsbox of 1591 with the inscription: 'Scripture doth record what to them is given is lent unto the Lord'

49

TYRANNY OF THE TITHE

C20 Tithe Memorial opposite Elmsett St Peter IP7 6PJ

The memorial was erected opposite the church gate in 1935 and marks a time when relations between the church and the community were very strained

Tithe means one tenth and traditionally farmers were required to give one tenth of their produce annually to the clergy. In 1836 this was converted into a cash payment but the rate was fixed when times were good and not adjusted when prices plummeted in 1931. The church refused to accept a lower sum. Charles Westren of Elmsett Hall could not pay. Bailiffs were sent in to seize his furniture and other goods. The whole village rallied to support him and the London bailiffs were frightened off. Following considerable 'civil disobedience' the law was changed in 1936 but it was not until 1976 that the tithe was abolished.

The inscription on the memorial reads: '1934. To commemorate the Tithe seizure at Elmsett Hall of furniture including baby's bed and blankets, herd of dairy cows, eight corn stacks and seed stacks valued at £1200 for tithe valued at £385.'

Discover more...

- Delightful porch with its C13 timbers, sheltering a door that is even older
- Beautifully carved early C17 pulpit, once in St Mary-at-Quay, Ipswich
- C17 communion rails
- The 1609 memorial in the chancel to Edward Sherland with symbols of death including a scythe and hourglass, and with two grinning skulls beneath
- The two sided Royal Coat of Arms of Queen Anne (1702-14) was re-dated 1757 for King George II. On the back are the Prince of Wales feathers

BENCH END THAT MOCKS THE MONKS

C14 'Edmund' bench end at Hadleigh St Mary IP7 5DU

Tradition has it that the head of St Edmund was found after his execution and then guarded by a wolf. This bench end in the south chapel depicts the legend of the finding of the head of the martyred St Edmund in the jaws of a wolf and at the same time is thought to be a caricature of the clergy. The neck is encircled with a collar, representing the ornament that used to be worn by monks in the reign of Richard II on their robes, while its back is covered with folded wings. Its back feet are cloven and its shoes at the front were those in common use at the end of the C14.

Discover more...

- Stained glass window in the south chapel portraying the story of Rowland Taylor, burned to death in 1555 in the reign of Queen Mary for his devotion to the Reformation

- Memorial to Hugh Rose who convened the famous Hadleigh Conference in the Deanery Tower in July 1833, spawning the Oxford Movement. This was a catholic revival within the Church of England and its adherents were known as Tractarians from publishing 'Tracts for the Times' to spread their beliefs

- The oldest spire in the county, soaring 71 ft above the 64 ft tower, has a clock bell cast around 1280

- The award-winning Porch Project that sprung from young people using the porch as a meeting place. They now meet regularly inside the church

51

GLIMPSE OF A GLORIOUS SCREEN

Remains of C15 rood screen at Kersey St Mary IP7 6EF

All that remains of this gorgeous C15 rood screen is a small panel resting against the north wall inside the church. The original screen would have spanned the width of the church, dividing the nave from the chancel. On top would have been the rood loft containing the rood itself — a figure of the crucified Christ with statues of the Virgin Mary and St John the Evangelist to either side. Outside you can see the bulge in the wall indicating where the rood stairway was. The fragment of the painted and decorated screen shows prophets and kings including St Edmund holding his arrow. The mutilations carried out in the 1640s allow us only a tantalising glimpse at what must have been a glorious and inspiring aid to worship at a time when there was not much beauty in the lives of ordinary people.

Discover more...

- The south porch with its superb flint flushwork outside and fine timber roof roofs, plastered over and only discovered in 1927
- The lectern with its C15 base surmounted by an eagle, probably 16C
- In the chancel the C14 carved stone arches for the piscina, a stone basin for draining away the water used in the Mass, and sedilia, seats for the priest and assistants. The carving was never completed, perhaps an indication of the ravages of the Black Death around 1349

NORMAN HERITAGE REVEALED

Norman arch at Polstead St Mary CO6 5BS

Here in this lovely little Norman church on a hill overlooking the Box valley is indeed 'hidden treasure'. Inside, at the west end, open the tower door, walk through and turn round. Here you will see the original western facade with its magnificent Norman arch through which you would have entered the church. Constructed in the C12, it is of stone, rounded, broad and handsomely decorated with zigzag mouldings, typical of the period.

This splendid arch is the precursor to a very special interior as you emerge into the nave to see more Norman work but of a different nature, the arcades being made from a rare mixture of bricks and blocks of a porous limestone called tufa. In fact, the bricks have set the scholars arguing but the most likely explanation is that, in about 1200AD, the bricks were made on site in Polstead and that puts them among the earliest surviving English bricks.

Discover more...

- The stone spire, the only surviving medieval one in Suffolk
- The font with its unusual brick bowl and a cover designed by an Oxford nun who was trained at the Slade School of Fine Art
- C17 Laudian communion rails surrounding the altar on three sides, originally designed to keep dogs out!

53

THE JAMESTOWN CONNECTION

American plaque dedicated to Gosnold's sister at Shelley All Saints IP7 5QX

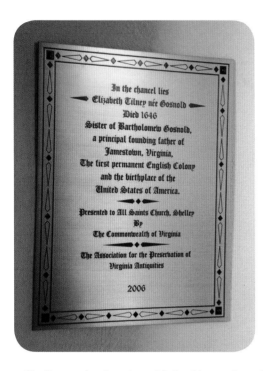

In the chancel lies
Elizabeth Tilney née Gosnold
Died 1646
Sister of Bartholomew Gosnold,
a principal founding father of
Jamestown, Virginia,
The first permanent English Colony
and the birthplace of the
United States of America.

Presented to All Saints Church, Shelley
By
The Commonwealth of Virginia

The Association for the Preservation of
Virginia Antiquities

2006

This bronze plaque on the chancel wall was given to the church by the Commonwealth of Virginia and the Association for the Preservation of Virginia Antiquities.

The story began when a broken slab was discovered under tiles near the vestry door in 2005. It had lost its inscription but experts believed it might have been the C17 grave of Elizabeth Tilney, sister of Suffolk explorer Bartholomew Gosnold. Captain Gosnold was involved in the first English settlement of Jamestown but died shortly after the arrival of the colonists in 1607.

In an attempt to help establish the identity of a skeleton found at Jamestown, thought to be Gosnold, the Church of England allowed the removal of DNA from the grave at Shelley — the first time this had been done for scientific reasons. No match was established so doubts still linger on as to the actual identities of the two skeletons. Even so there is evidence that Elizabeth Gosnold Tilney was indeed buried in the chancel at Shelley.

Registers at neighbouring Higham St Mary tell us that on 10 April, 1646, Elizabeth, widow of Thomas Tylney Esquire died 'and was burfied in Shelley chauncell the day followinge'.

Discover more...

- Elizabeth Gosnold married Thomas Tilney whose brother Philip had a fine tomb made for their mother Dame Margaret Tilney which can be seen beneath the north nave window
- C13 lancet (slit) window in the south wall of the chancel, reconstructed in 2000 to commemorate the millennium
- Tudor benches as part of the choir stalls with carved griffins and shields

THE DOORS COVERED WITH SAINTS

Carved south doors at Stoke by Nayland St Mary CO6 4QU

These rare and exquisitely carved south doors were made in the C15. Standing 10 ft 5 ins high and over 6 ft wide, they are covered with the figures of saints, birds and insects in canopied niches, intricately carved in oak. Pride of place goes to the Virgin Mary at the apex of the doors contained within a canopied niche with angels on either side bowing to her. It is thought that the main figures may represent a 'Tree of Jesse' with Old Testament ancestors of Jesus and his mother at the top. The 12 figures round the borders may well be the 12 apostles.

The glorious porch, with the parochial library above, has a central boss on the ceiling which again shows the Virgin Mary, thus are visitors welcomed to the church by the patron saint.

Discover more...

- The soaring 120 ft tower painted more than once by John Constable who wrote that the tower impressed on the surrounding county 'its own sacred dignity of character'
- The breathtaking height of the tower arch, best seen facing west from the chancel
- Fine brasses, including that of Catherine Howard, great grandmother to two of Henry VIII's wives, who died in 1465 and that of Sir William de Tendring who fought alongside Henry V at Agincourt. The alliance of the Howards and Tendrings by marriage can be seen in the combined Howard-de Tendring arms throughout the church, a reminder that the money for rebuilding the church came from these powerful families

THE MEDIEVAL BELL CAGE

C16 bell cage at East Bergholt St Mary CO7 6TE

This intriguing bell cage was built in the churchyard in 1531 as a temporary measure to house the bells when the building of the tower ceased in 1530.

The tower was started in 1525 and the question remains: Did the powerful and Suffolk-born Cardinal Wolsey offer to help pay for it before his downfall or did the Reformation put paid to the ambitious plans for a glorious tower when the wealth of parishes went to the Crown?

Whatever the reason, a remarkable bell cage now stands on the north side of the church and the bells, which rest in heavy wooden frames, are surrounded by walkways on which the ringers stand.

These great bells are unlike any other 'full circle' ring of bells anywhere in the world as they are rung using skilled force of hand rather than with ropes. The mighty tenor bell weighs over a ton.

Discover more...

- Note the range of building materials. The north side is almost entirely of brick whereas the south side and the tower base are of knapped flint. It is a good example of the stops and starts in church building that reflected the way wealthy benefactors came and went

- The Arts and Crafts style west window by Hugh Arnold who was killed in 1915. The reason it features the three mitres of the Diocese of Norwich is that the window was installed in 1905, nine years before the creation of the Diocese of St. Edmundsbury and Ipswich

- The ruined base of the tower which would have been visible for miles had it been completed

A JUBILEE LYCH GATE

C19 Arts and Crafts lych gate at Brantham St Michael and All Angels CO11 1PZ

The Old English Lich means corpse and the original lych or lich gate provided shelter for the shrouded corpse to be placed on a bier. The 1549 prayer book required the priest to meet the corpse at the gate where he would conduct the first part of the funeral service. Few medieval lych gates have survived but many, like this one, were erected in the C19 to commemorate a person or an event.

Designed by Edward Schroder Prior in the Arts and Crafts style this lych gate was given by Colonel Montague Browning, of Brantham Court to celebrate the Diamond Jubilee of Queen Victoria in 1897. It sits comfortably in its flint retaining walls and, because it curves gently in several planes, it creates a charming feeling of airiness. The heavy timbers are decorated with surprisingly delicate, carved, trailing leaves. The ridge beams boasts six patriotic and more substantial roses.

There are two inscriptions, one a reminder of the presence of God and the other recording the jubilee.

Discover more...

- The carved oak pulpit, another Arts and Crafts piece on which the Tree of Life is carved across three panels and given by a parishioner in 1900

- A copy of one of the three altar pieces 'Christ and the Children', painted in about 1804 by the famous landscape painter John Constable who was born in nearby East Bergholt. The original is at Emmanuel College Cambridge

- The C14 font, brought in from the church of St Martin at Palace, Norwich

CITY CHANCEL IN A COUNTRY CHURCH

C18 classical chancel at Shotley St Mary the Virgin IP9 1ES

Right up until the C20, the rector of a parish was traditionally responsible for maintaining the chancel of his church.

In 1745, the then rector, the Hon Henry Hervey (who later adopted his wife's family name of Aston) decided to replace the medieval structure with the rare period piece you see today. It adjoins the nave with an off-centre dark wooden arch displaying the Aston arms: a somewhat different focus from the more usual rood screen.

The walls are partly panelled, the windows contain clear glass, there are three-sided altar rails, and the barrel-vaulted ceiling has angels gazing down on the lavishly carved and painted reredos displaying sacred texts and portraits of Moses and Aaron.

Discover more...

- Medieval hammerbeam roof in the nave. In 2003 when the chancel roof was being repaired, medieval roof timbers matching those in the nave, were found above the visible ceiling
- Seating and pulpit made in 1874 by Robert Hawkins from Monks Eleigh
- Original barrel organ unusually converted into a conventional finger organ ensuring that the instrument remains in use even after 153 years
- Notice the stump of a tower. Made of septaria dredged from the local estuary, the rest of it fell down around 1630
- The large number of naval graves in the churchyards, including those of boys from the now closed HMS Ganges who died in accidents and two world wars

A POIGNANT JOURNEY

Stations of the Cross in slate at Felixstowe St John the Baptist IP11 7PL

The - usually 14 - Stations of the Cross have helped Christians over the centuries to follow the sad journey of Jesus Christ on Good Friday from his death-sentence to his death. St John's has 16, including the scene of Jesus entrusting Mary to the Apostle John's care and His rising from the dead.

Created by former worshipper and chorister Anthea Chalkley, the scenes are simply and beautifully etched on pieces of grey slate, mostly fixed to the arcade pillars. They were completed in 2005.

Pictured is the Station 'Jesus meets his Mother'. The prayer St John's has adopted for this Station is: 'We remember and pray for all women who are exploited and abused. For those who live their lives as slaves.'

A helpful leaflet is provided to help you view each Station in sequence, beginning in the north aisle and finishing in the Lady Chapel.

Discover more...

- Tower and spire built in 1914 by Charles Blomfield and soaring over 130 feet above this seaside town
- Colourful glass, mostly by James Powell & Sons, in almost every window enhance this devotional interior. John Betjeman wrote. 'I hurry past a cake shop's tempting scones, Bound for the red brick twilight of St John's'
- Font cover by Ipswich craftsman Harry Turner in 1912
- 1920s Lady Chapel gates featuring angels with St Gabriel and the Virgin Mary
- James Powell's mosaic reredos, framed with alabaster, showing the Last Supper, with the traitor Judas absent from the table

59

BOX PEWS WITH A BIBLE FOCUS

Plain box pews at Ramsholt All Saints IP12 3AE

The nave and part of the chancel of this beautifully-situated riverside church are filled with plain box pews, gathered round the two-decker pulpit, with the clerk's desk in the adjacent pew.

In the chancel, the seats face west towards the pulpit, rather than east towards the altar. This is a reminder that for 300 years it was Bible teaching rather than Holy Communion that was the focus of Anglican worship.

The fact that these pews were made around 1857 when most churches were throwing out this style of seating in favour of benches and choir stalls, indicated a reluctance to follow the new ordering of church furnishings that came with Victorian restorations. Clearly the new-fangled ideas of the Gothic Revival had not reached this remote church down a long cul-de-sac.

Discover more...

- Glorious views over the River Deben
- Eccentric, oval and buttressed tower with some parts perhaps dating back 1000 years though the windows were installed in the 1200s
- Stone coffin of the C13, unearthed near the tower in the 1850s
- Plaque on the north wall that tells of the Revd Henry Canham's democratic and most unusual action upon his departure from the parish in 1879

LIGHT OF THE WORLD

C21 altar frontal at Alderton St Andrew IP12 3BT

This fine altar frontal was designed by Lida Lopes Cardozo Kindersley and made by Maureen Rasmussen in 2004. Its theme is 'the light of the world' and the fish symbolise St Andrew to whom the church is dedicated. Andrew was one of the 12 Apostles of Jesus and a fisherman by trade.

The simple and elegant design of this work is typical of the style of Lida Lopes Cardozo who runs the Cardozo Kindersley Workshop in Cambridge, known for beautiful lettering on a range of materials.

Small areas of jewel-like colours represent the colours of the seasons of the Church's year.

Discover more...

- Ivy-clad ruins of a once-mighty tower which most recently fell in 1821, killing a cow in the churchyard
- Woodwose and dragon to greet you in the stone archway of the medieval porch
- The nave was restored to its former glory in the 1860s and the chancel rebuilt
- Royal arms of King George III
- Fine war memorial on the south wall of the nave
- Well-designed, moveable modern pews by Luke Hughes, furniture designer of Covent Garden and creator of the 'stackable pew'

RARE DISPLAY OF CHURCH PLATE

Holy Communion treasures on show at Woodbridge St Mary IP12 4LP

In this noble and beautiful church, there is a rare chance to examine treasures that are usually locked away in safes or bank vaults.

The latest security technology has enabled St Mary's to display church silver and other plate beneath the tower as part of the church's C21 reordering.

Here, craftsmanship in metal from the past 400 or so years may be enjoyed at close quarters, including chalices (cups), flagons (jugs) and patens (plates) used at Holy Communion, private communion sets used by clergy in the homes of sick people, and a silver shell for Baptisms.

Discover more...

- Magnificent tower, soaring 109 feet above the historic town
- Exquisite north porch, with an array of flint flushwork
- The seven sacraments, set in rays, on the C15 font
- Painted panels from the 1450s screen and from its 1898 replacement
- A kaleidoscope of C19 glass and the C20 east window by Martin Travers

THE CURIOUS BENCH ENDS

Carved bench ends at Hollesley All Saints IP12 3RE

The oak bench ends are a mixture of the original C15 examples in the north aisle and high-quality C20 replicas in the nave designed by former diocesan architect Henry Munro Cautley and carved by Harry Brown, an Ipswich craftsman, between 1949 and 1966.

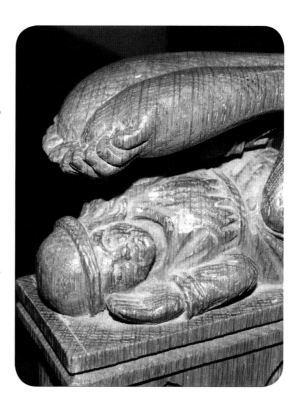

You can read more on the brass plaque on the back of the fifth pew on the south side which commemorates the Queen's coronation in 1953.

Other pews have representations of the Seven Deadly Sins and various animals, including a boar and the mythical sciapod with his enormous feet protecting himself from the heat of the sun, copied from the only medieval version at Dennington.

Discover more...

- Ancient south doorway dating from about 1300 but moved eastwards when Herbert J Green restored the church in 1886. Before this it was surrounded by a dilapidated porch where the nave and tower join, which is why the holy water basin, called a 'stoup,' is in the tower buttress
- When the north aisle was added in 1886, they discovered an early C13 arcade indicating an original aisle
- The stongly-coloured Holy Family window created by Welsh artist Meg Lawrence in the 1980s; detail right

63

THE RUINED NORMAN CHANCEL

Roofless remains of a Norman chancel at Orford St Bartholomew IP12 2LN

When King Henry II decided to build a castle in Orford in the 1160s, the riverside settlement got its first church. You can wander through the roofless remains of the original Norman chancel to the east of the present C14 church and distinctive Norman carving can still be seen on the mighty round piers of the chancel arcade.

When the nave was rebuilt, the Norman chancel was still attached but, as Orford declined economically, the chancel fell into ruin and was abandoned and walled off.

Since about 1710, the nave and aisles have served as the complete church. This, together with the south aisle being exceptionally wide, has resulted in a virtually square church.

In the Lady Chapel within the church, you can see more architectural details of the old Norman church.

Discover more...

- The sturdy tower rebuilt in the 1960s after it fell in 1830
- The typical C15 Suffolk eight-sided font
- West door made in 1928 by Archdeacon Darling and his carving class (see Eyke, Treasure 67) to a design by pioneer woman architect Hilda Mason
- The round slate floor plaque recording the first performances of four of Benjamin Britten's church operas
- In the Lady Chapel the C21 bronze lamp in the form of a crown of thorns, designed and made by Orford artist Tim Fargher

RARE ANGLO SAXON CARVING

The Saxon cross shaft at Iken St Botolph IP12 2ES

This rare piece of Anglo Saxon carving lay hidden for centuries in the stonework of the tower of this ancient pilgrim church. Remarkably, it was used simply as a reinforcement when the tower was built in the C15.

Originally this beautiful cross was at least nine feet tall, although less than five feet remains. Although very worn, its four surfaces have remarkable carvings, including a creature with an open mouth, a long tongue and a coiled body.

The C9 cross shaft takes us back to the early days of Christianity in Suffolk when Saint Botolph became the abbot of the monastery founded here in AD654. This cross probably marked the site as a holy place and commemorated St Botolph and his church after the Danes destroyed it.

Discover more...

- C14 nave, beautifully restored after a fire in 1968
- Victorian chancel built of Kentish ragstone to the designs of John Whichcord of Maidstone
- Reredos of the Last Supper and carvings of farm animals and wildlife
- Stunning view of the river Alde from the north side of the church

65

THE ASCENSION WINDOW

Late C20 east window at Chillesford St Peter IP12 3PX

Designed by Surinder Warboys of Mellis, Suffolk this is one of the most striking modern stained glass windows in Suffolk.

The artist's work is about orchestrating light and colour and the vivid blues of this glass are dramatically reflected across the plain white walls of this ancient little church.

The window was commissioned by parishioners in 1991 after the previous Victorian glass depicting the Gospels was destroyed in a tragic incident.

In the artist's words 'the window is a celebration of life inspired by the Ascension'.

The altar fontal and lectern hangings, designed by Isobel Clover and worked by Margaret Cuddiford, echo the vibrant colours of this amazing work.

Discover more...

- Tower built in the C14 from local corraline crag - containing fossilised shells - from pits on the Orford peninsular
- C13 font of Purbeck marble from Dorset
- Squints in the walls between nave and chancel for viewing the high altar
- Victorian west window in the tower by Edward Frampton showing Christ walking on the water

A NORMAN CROSSING TOWER

Central crossing arches of Eyke All Saints IP12 2QL

This curious church is dominated internally by what remains of a central Norman crossing tower.

The upper part of the tower has disappeared, leaving the magnificent four broad and low Norman arches which once formed the base of the tower.

The arches on the east and west sides are decorated with chevron or zigzag patterns which are characteristic of Norman architecture. The other two arches are narrower and plain. The present nave and chancel of the C14 replace the Norman originals.

Discover more...

- Octagonal C15 font with four lions around the shaft and symbols of the four Evangelists with Tudor roses on the bowl
- Brass of about 1420 of John Staverton (in judicial robes) and his wife on the north wall. He was Baron of the Exchequer under Henry VI
- Replica of a C15 key, the 'ward' forming the letters IKE for 'Eyke'. The original is in the British Museum
- Delightful bench ends, including a penguin and a snake, made by Archdeacon Darling and local people he trained in wood carving classes when he was rector 1893-1938. He also made most of the other furniture

67

THE SOARING FONT COVER

18 ft font cover at Ufford St Mary of the Assumption IP13 6DW

This spectacular, telescopic font cover has been described as 'the most beautiful in the world' by author and architect Henry Munro Cautley.

It was created around 1450, probably by local workmen under a master designer, and restored to its full beauty in the 1980s.

Even the infamous iconoclast, William Dowsing, who saw and spared it in 1643, wrote of 'a glorious cover over the font, like a Pope's triple crown, a pelican on the top pricking its breast, all gilt over with gold', though it is thought this may have been more scathing than admiring.

But it remains today as a testament to the exquisite workmanship and attention to detail that past generations lavished on their local churches.

Discover more...

- Scratch dials on the buttress beside the C13 priest's doorway, marking the hour when Mass was said
- Grand porch featuring 'flushwork' of knapped flint, built around 1475
- Late C15 benches with remarkable carved ends
- Massive monument to Sir Henry Wood, who died 1671 and was Treasurer to the household of Queen Henrietta Maria
- St Leonard's chapel – fitted out as a War Memorial in 1919 by Sir Ninian Comper; his east window showing a British soldier and sailor helping Jesus to carry his cross

THE SANCTUARY RING

The door handle at Burgh St Botolph IP13 6QB

The remarkable door handle of the inner door takes the form of an iron ring set on a heavily bossed backplate said to have been forged in the C13. On the ring you may be able to see the outlines of two lizards – ancient emblems of good fortune.

In medieval times, people seeking refuge from justice could take sanctuary within a church. Holding on to the ring would give them that protection.

St Botolph, the missionary monk, may have planted Christianity here in the 600s or 700s; it is said that his bones were later brought here for safety from the Danes.

Discover more...

- The carvings on the eight-sided font –symbols of the four Evangelists, two angels and two representations of the Annunciation

- The pulpit dated 1708, though in an earlier, Jacobean, style
- Beautiful collection of stained glass windows by the late Victorian designer Charles Kempe
- A painting by Anna Zinkeisen illustrating all the birds in the Bible in memory of her husband who died in 1967
- The headstone in the churchyard (just east of the vestry) of John and Mary Steptoo (she died in 1756), has a pickaxe, spade, coffin and hourglass – all symbols of our mortality

69

RICHLY EMBELLISHED ALTAR SCREEN

The C19 altar reredos at Swilland St Mary IP6 9LP

The heavily gilded altar screen or reredos is reminiscent of the elaborate interiors of churches before the C16 English Reformation when such sights were more common but this piece is dated 1894 and in the style of George Bodley, leading Gothic Revival architect of the C19.

It shows the influence of the Revd Robert Hoffman Faulconer who beautified the church in the Anglo-Catholic tradition during that period.

Niches are filled with four groups of five small gilded figures of Apostles and Saints surrounding a central Crucifixion. At the lower level are four crowned MRs for Mary Regina, Queen of Heaven, and six winged angels. The whole is decorated in gold and Marian blue, the colour associated with the Virgin Mary

Discover more...

- Massive Norman south doorway, dating from the 1100s
- Tower of C16 brick, topped with eccentric Victorian belfry of 1897, with gabled roof and copper-covered spirelet
- Royal arms of Queen Anne carved in lime wood
- Stained glass nave windows (1890s) of Saints Felix, Edmund and Richard

TRIBUTE TO THOMAS CLARKSON

Memorials to Thomas Clarkson (anti-slavery pioneer) at Playford St Mary IP6 9DS

The massive obelisk in the graveyard is to Thomas Clarkson 'Friend of Slaves' and was erected in 1857 'by a few surviving friends'.

Thomas Clarkson worked with William Wilberforce and others to persuade Parliament to abolish the slave trade, leading to the Acts of 1807 and 1833. Clarkson died at Playford Hall in 1846 and is buried in the churchyard just outside the priest's door on the south side of the chancel.

Inside the church on the south wall is a further memorial of 1878 incorporating a bust portrait in profile by Sir Hamo Thornycroft. Not surprisingly, there are other memorials to Clarkson, including in his birthplace, Wisbech and at Westminster Abbey.

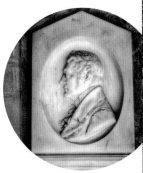

THOMAS CLARKSON
THE FRIEND OF SLAVES

ERECTED 1857,
BY A FEW SURVIVING FRIENDS.

Discover more...

- Late C14 tower to the south of the nave – one of the grandest Suffolk south porch towers
- Magnificent military brass in the chancel of Sir George Felbrigg who built the tower and died in 1400. Lord of the Manor and Esquire at Arms to King Edward III, his effigy is almost five feet tall
- Memorial to Sir George Biddell Airy, the Astronomer Royal who died in 1892 and is buried at Playford where he had a cottage since 1845

LEGEND OF OUR LADY OF IPSWICH

The statue that re-established a C12 shrine at Ipswich St Mary at the Elms IP1 2AA

Ipswich was a prosperous port with 39 churches in the C12. Among them was St Mary's Chapel containing a famous and beautiful carved wooden statue of Mary and Jesus.

In 1297, 'Our Lady of Grace' was the scene of a Royal wedding when Princess Elizabeth, the daughter of Edward I, married the Count of Holland in the shrine. There were also visits by Henry VII, Catherine of Aragon, Sir Thomas More and Cardinal Thomas Wolsey, who was born in Ipswich.

In September 1538, during the Reformation, the statue - known as both Our Lady of Grace and Our Lady of Ipswich - was taken to London to be burnt.

The story goes that English Catholic sailors rescued it and transported it to the Italian seaside town of Nettuno. This could well be the case because an old wooden statue at Nettuno known as 'The English Lady or 'Our Lady of the Graces' is considered by experts to be one and the same.

What you see in the church is an oak replica of the Nettuno statue carved by local artist Robert Mellamphy and placed here in 2002 to re-establish the Shrine of our Lady of Grace at Ipswich.

Discover more...

- The site of the original shrine was marked in 1990 by a bronze statue by Robert Mellamphy in Lady Lane, a short distance from St Mary at the Elms
- The Tudor tower said to be constructed with bricks brought from the Netherlands by Cardinal Wolsey to use at his projected college. Wolsey's Gate in College Street is all that remains of the college
- St Mary's cottage, just north of the churchyard, is dated 1467 and said to be the oldest occupied house in Ipswich

TOWN'S PANORAMA IN A MEMORIAL

William Smart's memorial of 1599 at Ipswich St Mary le Tower IP1 3BN

If you have ever wondered what Ipswich would have looked like in medieval times, you can see the earliest known panorama of the town at its civic church of St Mary le Tower.

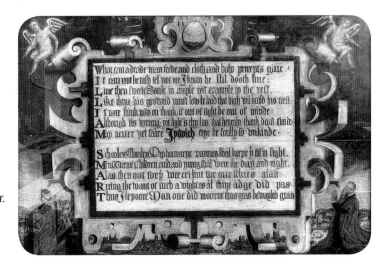

William Smart was MP for Ipswich at the time of the Spanish Armada and a benefactor of the town and his memorial has an epitaph in verse which contains an acrostic or word puzzle which has in it the key to the earliest known panorama of Ipswich painted beneath the verses.

The view is over Stoke and Broomhill on the left and Bishop's Hill on the right.

Details of visible landmarks include eight churches, a monastery, a mill and a stream which is in fact the Gipping. Also featured are pictures of William and his wife Alice.

The memorial, which is oil painted on board, can be seen on the north wall opposite the south entrance.

Discover more...

- Wrought iron stands for the ceremonial sword and maces of Ipswich Borough and the Corporation pews for this is the civic church of Ipswich
- The marquetry panel and the curving stairway of the late C17 pulpit
- Early C15 font with the lions sitting on human heads
- The 12 apostles and 12 angels on the choir stalls
- Medieval bench ends of churchwardens pews at the back of the church
- The grand and gilded reredos or altarpiece of 1895

AN OUTSIZE CHANCEL

C20 extension at Rushmere St Andrew IP5 1DH

St Andrew's is not the straightforward medieval building that it first appears to be. A north aisle was added in 1861 when the nave and chancel were rebuilt to the design of Edward Hakewill. Then in the C20 came a radical enlargement of the chancel, dramatically doubling its capacity, and enabling it to serve a community that has grown to about 10,000. George Pace of York was the architect employed to create this brand new space in 1967 and today the visitor can see how modern materials and construction techniques have taken their place beside more traditional workmanship.

The central altar provides a focus for worshippers and much of the seating is movable to allow a range of activities. It is a perfect example of the need for church buildings to evolve appropriately.

Discover more...

- Medieval tower which was heightened at the end of the C15, thanks to the generosity of William and Katherine Cayde
- Lovely C19 bench ends carved by William Polley of Coggeshall. Can you find the angels holding models of the tower and the chancel and the animals with the symbols of Saints Matthew, Mark, Luke and John?

AN ALTAR HIDDEN IN THE WALL

Rediscovered altar at Pettistree St Peter and St Paul IP13 0HP

You will often see a niche in the stone walls of a church chancel, near the altar, with a small drain. This is a piscina, used to allow the water used in the Mass to drain into consecrated or sanctified ground.

At Pettistree, the piscinas on both the north and south walls of the nave were a clear indication of where altars would have stood before the radical changes of the C16 Reformation so it was no great surprise in 2005 when a rare stone altar slab featuring four of its five consecration crosses, was uncovered in the south wall.

Why was it hidden in this way? Quite simply, when all stone altars had to be broken up and replaced by wooden tables 'by law' in the 1540s, some churches quietly buried or hid these sacred pieces of stone. The five crosses represent the five wounds of Jesus on the cross – in his hands, feet and side, reminding the priest at the altar that (as St Paul said) he was 'proclaiming the Lord's death until he comes again'.

Discover more...

- C13 monochrome glass in the east window on the south side of the broad chancel – some of the oldest in Suffolk
- Brasses of Francis Bacon and his two wives dated 1580 on the south wall of the chancel
- Charity board of 1717 on west wall providing for bread to be supplied to 'such poor of the parish as shall here religiously and constantly joyn with ye Congregation ... in prayers...'

75

PRECIOUS SURVIVAL OF FURNISHINGS

C17 and C18 chancel furnishings at Hoo St Andrew and St Eustachius IP13 7QT

In a church service, you will often hear the words 'Draw near with faith.' as the priest invites the congregation to share in 'the body and blood of Christ'. These are the words of the 1662 Book of Common Prayer and the simple chancel furnishings at Hoo provide the perfect example of the setting in which this Christian ritual was performed during that period.

Here you will find communion rails to protect the sacred space where Holy Communion takes place. A small, late C17 communion table was used by the priest to serve the consecrated bread and wine to the communicants who would use the bench against the south wall. At that time, with the greater emphasis on Bible teaching, this would be only three or four times a year. The same table is used for Holy Communion today.

Discover more...

- Note the unique dedication of the church that links the apostle St Andrew with a C2 Roman soldier martyr. Discover the modern icons of both saints on the pulpit
- The six mighty tie-beams supporting the ceiling, one dated 1595
- A Tudor rose among the carvings on the much-defaced C15 font
- A rough iron-bound parish chest dating back to around 1300 by the north door

SAXON STONES IN THE TOWER

The Saxon/Norman tower base at Debenham St Mary IP14 6QN

If you want to know more about how people tackled stone masonry almost 1000 years ago, try to visit this church where you can see the classic Saxon 'long and short' work at the western corners of the tower. You can clearly see how the dressed stones, known as quoins, alternate between horizontal and vertical which is the way our ancient forbears worked.

The lower parts of this tower are thought to date from the period in the C11 in which the Saxon and Norman styles of architecture overlap, the arch towards the nave having distinctive Norman features.

The upper part of the tower dates from the C14 and it lost some 20 feet when it was struck by lightning in 1667.

Discover more...

- The large two-storied porch added to the western face of the tower in the C14
- Striking floor of local red and yellow bricks laid in a herringbone pattern in 1871
- Elaborate marble effigy by the south door to the Revd John Simson who died in 1697
- Medieval parish chest with three locks and iron bands with decorative terminals in scroll and leaf and anchor patterns
- Curious 1911 fretwork rendering of the Lord's Prayer on the north wall of the nave
- Rare coffin plate of Sir Charles Gawdy by the priest's door in the chancel. He died in 1650 and was 'blessed in the happie choice of a most virtuous wife.'

TOMBS OF A TUDOR DYNASTY

The Howard monuments at Framlingham St Michael IP13 9AZ

When Henry VIII was on the throne, you couldn't get much closer to the Tudor Royals than the Dukes of Norfolk and here they are in all their funerary splendour in the vast chancel of this beautiful church.

The whole character of medieval St Michael's changed when Thomas Howard, third Duke of Norfolk, decided to build a chancel at the east end as a mausoleum for his family tombs when Henry did away with Thetford Priory, their original resting place. The Duke was uncle to two of the King's wives, Anne Boleyn and Catherine Howard, and his daughter Mary married the King's illegitimate (and favourite) son Henry Fitzroy, Duke of Richmond. Their magnificent tomb can be seen, along with the 3rd Duke's own elaborate tomb dating back to the 1530s.

The vibrant alabaster monument of 1614, pictured here, is to the Earl of Surrey, poet son of the third Duke who was beheaded on a dubious charge of treason in 1547. That's why his coronet lies beside his knee rather than on his head.

Discover more...

- The 'Flodden Helm', high above the 3rd Duke of Norfolk's tomb. The helmet was carried in the 2nd Duke's funeral procession as he was victor of the famous Battle of Flodden 500 years ago
- Historic organ, made by Thomas Thamar for Pembroke College, Cambridge in 1674, a rare and precious survival
- Remarkable painted Glory reredos below the east window, dating from the early C18

A SACRED SURVIVOR

Rare pyx canopy at Dennington St Mary IP13 8AA

Among the many treasures of Dennington, the rarest hangs above the high altar. It is a veiled medieval pyx canopy used to support the little pyx in which the consecrated bread of the Eucharist is reserved for communion of the sick and dying.

Dating from about 1500 and almost 5 ft tall, this slender, ornamented spire with traces of its original colouring, is the only pyx canopy complete enough to be used for its original purpose, though parts of three others can be found elsewhere in the country.

Having been used as a doorstop, this pyx canopy was restored to its rightful use in 1927 – a use which continues today.

Discover more...

- Rare medieval screens round the aisle chapels
- In vibrant colour, the tomb and superb alabaster effigies of William, Lord Bardolf, who fought at Agincourt and died in 1441, and his wife Joan
- Exceptional C15 carved benches in the rear part of the nave and aisles. Seek out the curious sciapod –a mythical creature with an enormous foot used to shield himself against the sun
- Beautifully carved font cover, with a little bird pecking at fruit at its summit
- Sand table in the north aisle on which the village children could learn to read and write in the C19

79

SEVEN SACRAMENT FONT

The Seven Sacrament font at Badingham St John the Baptist IP13 8JX

Fonts illustrating the seven sacraments of the medieval church are a speciality of Suffolk and Norfolk – and this is one of the very best. Starting from the east face and going round clockwise, the panels are: baptism (by immersion); matrimony; ordination; confirmation; Mass; penance; extreme unction; and, finally, baptism again – in this case the baptism of Christ with St John the Baptist pouring water over Our Lord's head. On the shaft are the figures of angels and bishops, with St Edmund to the south.

The font dates back to 1480 and the extreme unction panel of the last rites provides a glimpse of life in those times. A sick man is being anointed with holy oil while his wife weeps into a handkerchief. You can see his shoes and chamber pot by the bed.

Discover more...

- The C12 Norman corbels in the porch, one depicting a curious cat
- The floor that slopes upward towards the east by two feet or so
- The C15 nave roof – of which one expert has written: 'other roofs may be more elaborate but none can surpass (this) in technical skill and refinement of detail'
- The oversize tomb for lawyer William Cotton and his wife Lucie in the chancel with its Corinthian columns and life-sized effigies. It dates back to James I

THE HEADSTONE SUNDIAL

Sundial incorporated into headstone at Saxmundham St John the Baptist IP17 1ES

You will find this treasure to the west of the church, a short distance from the path.

Look for a group of four headstones but pay special attention to the one dedicated to John Noller who died in 1725 at the age of 58, and Mary his wife.

Small, rectangular recesses are cut on the diagonal into both the east and west faces of the stone.

The shadow cast by the top edge shows the time on the parallel hour lines carved within each rectangle. In this way, the headstone uniquely serves as a simple sundial.

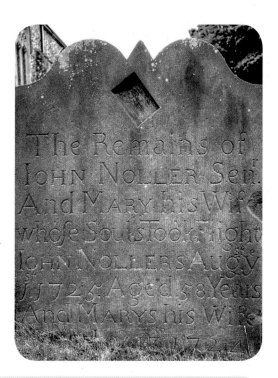

Discover more...

*   Entrance through the western face of the tower, replacing the original south porch as part of a radical rebuilding and restoration in 1872

*   Hammerbeam nave roof, revealed when the plaster ceiling was removed in 1932
*   Font of the C15 with lions and woodwoses (wild men) round the shaft and shields on the bowl, with Victorian cover surmounted by St John the Baptist
*   Ovals of C17 glass believed to come from Innsbruck in the east window of the south aisle and featuring saints and secular scenes
*   East window of the north aisle, designed and donated in 1872 by Saxmundham sisters, Mary and Bessie McKean

81

ROYAL ARMS TO REMEMBER

Royal Arms at Friston St Mary IP17 1PX

The enormous Royal Arms of King James I (1603-25) dominate this simple church. Over six feet square and carved from planks five inches thick, it was reassembled from pieces recovered from the tower in 1935 and attached to the north wall of the nave.

Royal Arms began to be displayed in churches under King Henry VIII, were banned by Queen Mary and again under the Commonwealth, but restored by King Charles II in 1660 who made them obligatory in every parish church.

Discover more...

- Tower, originally of the C14, rebuilt as a careful copy in 1900
- C17 table inside the doorway that was once the altar
- Cover of what was probably the church's first English Bible, from about 1550, displayed beside the Royal Arms
- The base of the C19 font is probably the original font bowl turned upside down
- Chancel walls and ceiling featuring C19 stencilled patterns

FOR THOSE IN PERIL

The lifeboat memorials at Aldeburgh St Peter and St Paul IP15 5BB

If you walk to the eastern edge of the large churchyard, on high ground overlooking the North Sea, you will find the monument and graves of the seven brave Aldeburgh men who were drowned in a tragic event that shook this seaside town on 7 December 1899.

The 'Aldeburgh' lifeboat, once thought unsinkable, capsized when she was struck broadside-on by two huge waves in heavy seas. While 12 of the 18-man crew were flung clear, six became trapped beneath the upturned boat and a seventh died later of his injuries.

A large copper plaque on the west wall just inside the door recalls the tragedy of those who lost their lives that night and quotes from the words of Psalm 77: *'Thy way is in the sea, and thy path in the great waters, and thy footsteps are not known'.*.

Discover more...

- While in the churchyard, seek out the graves of the great composer Benjamin Britten, the tenor Peter Pears, and Imogen Holst, composer, conductor, and only child of composer Gustav Holst
- Benjamin Britten memorial window by John Piper, illustrating the composer's Three Church Parables
- The bust of George Crabbe at the entrance to the north aisle chapel. Poet, surgeon and clergyman, he was born in the town, married in Beccles church, and died in 1832
- World War I memorial in the south aisle chapel, with radiant nimbus highlighting the inscription
- C20 glass in the east window of the south aisle by Archibald Nicholson featuring, among the saints, St Cecilia, patron saint of music

THE AIRSHIP RELICS IN THE PORCH

Relics of a Zeppelin airship from 1917 at Theberton St Peter IP16 4SA

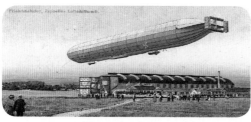

The relics of an airship are not normally what you would expect to find in a church porch but in June 1917, during WWI, a German Zeppelin L48 (an airship armed with bombs) was shot down by a British aircraft above the fields of a farm at Theberton. As the huge airship began to fall to earth, the glow in the sky could apparently be seen for miles around.

The 16 Germans who died in the crash were initially buried in the churchyard, but were later moved to the Cannock Chase German Military Cemetery in Staffordshire where German war graves have been consolidated.

Over the road in the graveyard extension to St Peter's, a memorial to the dead crew remains to this day. It reads, among other brief details: 'Who art thou that judges another man's servant?' (Romans 14:4).

Parts of the Zeppelin are preserved in the porch where you can read all about the drama of that early summer's morning.

Discover more...

- Round Norman tower with an octagonal bell stage
- Scratch dial on the east buttress of the porch for indicating the times of the Mass
- Stained glass memorial window on the north wall to Lieut. Col. Doughty-Wylie, VC, killed at Gallipoli – portraying him as St George with the vanquished dragon
- Welcoming table tomb of 1678 by south porch – 'Here is a stone to sit upon...'

EFFIGY OF A PRIEST

84

Brass of Sir Edmund de Brundish at Brundish St Lawrence IP13 8AY

Beneath the tomb recess in the north wall of the nave, though not in its original position, is the fine brass effigy of a priest, robed to celebrate the Holy Communion in about 1380 and showing the beauty and detail of his Eucharistic vestments. The inscription, in Norman French, tells us that he is 'Sire Esmound de Burnedishh', reminding us that priests were then given the title 'Sir' though it was simply a form of address rather than a knighthood.

This priest would surely be pleased to see this lonely 'church in the lanes' so beautifully restored over the past decade.

Discover more...

- Four more fine brasses, with intriguing effigies
- C15 benches, with worn poppyhead ends, some hidden by the box pews which were made in 1826
- Handsome pulpit with fine C17 tester or sounding-board, to throw the preacher's voice outwards rather than upwards
- The church's very first pipe organ, built by Peter Bumstead in 2010

85

THE JUBILEE FEASTS

Paintings at Worlingworth St Mary IP13 7NT

When Worlingworth throws a party, it does so in style – and dramatically records it for posterity.

On the south nave wall of this beautiful church hang two paintings. The first shows the Village Feast commemorating the Golden Jubilee of King George III in 1810 when an ox was roasted on a spit in the grounds of Worlingworth Hall. The second – pictured here – is of the celebration in 2002 for our present Queen's Golden Jubilee, held in exactly the same place.

The parishioners have never discovered who did the first painting and believe it was an itinerant Italian artist. The second was commissioned by two parishioners and is by John Raey from Lowestoft

You can even see the actual wooden spit in the church on which the ox was roasted for the 1810 feast.

Discover more...

- One of the finest C15 font covers in East Anglia, rising 20 feet into the air
- Glorious double hammerbeam roof spanning the entire width of the church, there being no side aisles
- Set of handsome C17 box pews dated to 1630
- The poignant brass plaque memorials to members of the French family, patrons of the church, who were killed in action in WW1
- The village fire engine, made in 1760

A STRANGE STONE OR A FOSSIL?

Remarkable flint in the tower at Wilby St Mary IP21 5LE

The sight of a carved head in the stonework of a church is one thing but quite another is the existence of a 'bird', thousands of years old, inhabiting the flintwork of Wilby's handsome 85-foot tower.

Set in the north wall, near the north-west buttress and about seven feet above the ground, is a flint which has been split to reveal its core, exposing the outline of a bird's head – its beak having a hooked end.

Whoever worked this remarkable flint into the masonry of the tower ensured it was prominently placed and the 'right way up', suggesting visitors to the church were meant to appreciate it.

Discover more...

- Magnificent 1400s porch, sheltering a medieval south door with its sanctuary ring to which those seeking refuge from justice would cling for protection (see Treasure 68)
- St Christopher wall painting facing you as you enter the church. Can you spot the fish?
- High quality carving of the medieval bench ends in north and south aisles
- Lovely fragments of medieval glass at the top of the nave windows
- Handsome, elaborately carved, C17 century pulpit

87

ST EDMUND AND THE WOLF

St Edmund bench end at Hoxne St Peter and St Paul IP21 5BE

For centuries Hoxne people have passed on the story that St Edmund met his terrible end after hiding from the Danes under the Goldbrook Bridge in 870.

The glint of his spurs in the River Lark is said to have alerted a newly married couple crossing the bridge who raised the alarm, thus enabling the Danes to capture him and demand he renounce his Christian faith. When he refused they are said to have tied him to a nearby oak to shoot arrows at him. Remaining steadfast he was beheaded and when his followers found him, his head was missing.

Tradition has it that Edmund's severed head was lovingly guarded by a wolf and on a C15 bench-end in the Lady Chapel of the church, the subject is skilfully and beautifully carved. Although Edmund's crowned and bearded head is well preserved, sadly the wolf's head has gone. His paws, however, are beautifully detailed.

Recent research suggests that Bradfield St Clare could be a more likely location for the martyrdom of Edmund but no doubt his name will always be linked with Hoxne.

Discover more...

- Remains of once spectacular wall-paintings of around 1400 above the arches of the C13 arcade
- The arms of the Bishop of Norwich and the Duke of Suffolk on the font bowl that dates back to the mid-C15
- Exhibition of Hoxne history and heritage in the north aisle

MASTERPIECE OF A FONT

Seven sacrament font at Cratfield St Mary IP19 0BU

Elevated on its two steps, this mutilated masterpiece of the late 1400s provided many visual aids to teach the Christian faith and it is at this font that the residents of Cratfield began, and still begin, their Christian journey.

Although the magnificent stone carving was defaced in 1644, you can still make out some of the 32 saints and angels round the stem and bowl as well as the characters in the panels where five of the seven sacraments remain. They are: anointing the sick, baptism, confirmation, ordination, and marriage. Mass and penance have been blanked out and the remaining eighth panel represents Christ crucified.

This is one of only 38 seven sacrament fonts in the country.

Discover more...

- C15 panelled nave roof
- Unusual sets of C17 benches in the side aisles
- Massive C15 chest, requesting prayers for Walter Walsh who gave it
- Unique medieval two-storey clock casing in the tower space and 1700s clock mechanism near the entrance

A LABOUR OF LOVE

Remarkable painted roof at Huntingfield St Mary the Virgin IP19 0PR

Some of the most extraordinary Victorian church decoration in the country can be found in this church in the depths of rural Suffolk and it is hard to imagine how it was all done by one woman.

The single hammerbeam roof is painted in vibrant colours featuring gilded angels with banners, crowns and shields and it is recorded that 225 books of gold leaf were used in the nave alone.

It was Mildred Holland, wife of rector William Holland, who recreated the splendour of a medieval roof in the chancel to awe and inspire the congregation. The church was closed for eight months from September 1859 to April 1860 while she completed her task, advised by E.L. Blackburne, an authority on medieval decoration.

In 1863 Mrs Holland started on the nave roof, featuring the 12 apostles, a labour of love that took a full three years. She worked alone, apparently lying on her back on scaffolding, and this in spite of the style of the tight corsets and many petticoats favoured by Victorian women.

Discover more...

- Memorial stones to William and Mildred Holland, who both died at Huntingfield, to the left of the entrance gates in the churchyard
- Traditional East Anglian font of late C14, very similar to that of Wingfield church and with a C19 cover modelled on the medieval one at Ufford
- Fragments of medieval glass in the east window of the south aisle including the de la Pole arms quartered with Wingfield as on the font
- C19 bench ends featuring the collared greyhounds, supporters of the Vanneck family who were great benefactors of the church

SECRET OF THE NORMAN TOWER

Room in the tower at Wissett St Andrew IP19 0JG

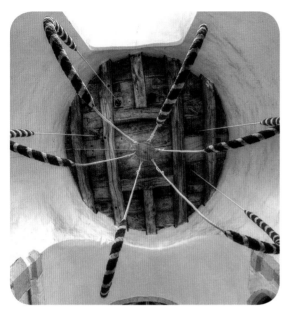

The handsome round church tower that has stood in the village of Wissett since the middle of the C12 is one of 40 in Suffolk but this one is of special interest.

The first floor room was used by the priest as living quarters when travelling from one parish to another and the ceiling has recently been analysed by tree ring and carbon dating, revealing that the trees used in its construction were felled between 1145 and 1205.

This astonishing information was uncovered during work on the tower to replace the bell frame and re-hang the bells. The work also uncovered a 'polishing' stone and a C16 woman's leather shoe – thought to ward off evil spirits in the days when Christian beliefs often combined with folk beliefs.

The tower itself has been described as a fine example of Norman architecture although round towers are not a specific feature of that period. All but 13 of the 175 in the country are in East Anglia where stone for corners was scarce and costly to ship in and flint from the fields was widely used.

Discover more...

- World War I wooden burial cross at the base of the inside of the tower
- Norman south doorway with carved beasts, including a cat, a bird and a crowned human head
- C20 oak pews with medieval poppyheads incorporated
- C20 statue of St Andrew by Peter Eugene Ball

DRAMA OF THE EASTER SEPULCHRE

Easter sepulchre at South Elmham St Margaret IP20 0PJ

The lovely arched recess in the north sanctuary wall, flanked by pinnacles and crowned with a finial, with a shelf beneath, resting upon beautifully carved stone panels, looks like a tomb recess in miniature. This is the Easter sepulchre where, every Good Friday, some of the consecrated bread from the Mass was placed with great solemnity and then brought back in triumph to the altar on Easter morning, dramatically symbolising the burial of Jesus in the tomb or sepulchre.

Many Easter sepulchres were portable wooden structures, although sometimes important people positioned their tombs where they could double as Easter sepulchres, as seen at Blythburgh and Long Melford.

Discover more...

- The two-storeyed porch, containing the village stocks
- The C15 arch-braced nave roof
- The tower staircase doorway, where John Sellynge has immortalised himself in C16 graffiti in the stonework

THE LATTICED EAST END

Rare east wall and window at Barsham Holy Trinity NR34 8HA

You'll need to walk round the outside of the church to view the extraordinary east wall with its criss-cross grid of stone, extending across the east window to form a pattern of lozenge shapes. Built in the late C16 or early C17, it serves the purpose of strengthening the east end and is thought to be unique in an English church, although nearby Spexhall's east wall of 1713 is similar.

The 'lozenge' pattern also forms the Etchingham coat of arms — lords of the manor from about 1420 to the 1540s — which may have inspired the Barsham builders to be 'different'.

From the inside of the church, you can admire the 28 saints in richly-coloured glass looking out from their lozenge frames, the work of the successful Victorian designer Charles Kempe in the 1870s.

Discover more...

- Devotional interior, largely created by Frederick Eden in the early 1900s, whose firm was responsible for most of the glass
- Tomb of Adrian Bell, the renowned C20 writer on Suffolk, near the south porch
- The Norman font bowl, now in the sanctuary, which was replaced in the 1400s
- The rare chancel screen of the early 1600s

93

A 'DECENT' ALTAR TABLE

Elizabethan communion table at Blyford All Saints IP19 9JY

Exquisitely carved with bulbous legs, this splendid piece of carpentry is widely regarded as one of the best altar tables of the late 1500s.

It is a real treasure in a small wayside church and is still used for its sacred purpose.

Under Edward VI, Nicholas Ridley, the reforming Bishop of London and elsewhere, ordered the removal of 'remote' stone altars, replacing them with wooden altar tables that worshippers could stand or kneel round to receive the sacrament – the bread and the wine of Holy Communion.

In November 1550, the Privy Council ordered all Bishops to follow Ridley's example in replacing a church's stone altar with a 'decent table'. This one is very decent indeed!

As for Ridley, a supporter of Lady Jane Grey's claim to the throne, he was burned at the stake during the reign of Catholic Queen Mary.

Discover more...

- Two fine Norman doorways of around 1100 in the nave
- The wooden cross from Captain Walter Day's grave in Flanders, where he was killed in 1916 at the age of 31
- C13 piscina built into the angle of the window near the altar. The piscina is a stone basin used to drain away the water used in the Mass
- A fine 1400s porch with elaborate patterns of split flint known as flushwork
- A banner-stave locker in the wall, where banners used in processions were stored

WHAT THE RAIN REVEALED

Doom painting at Wenhaston St Peter IP19 9EG

This astonishing painting on oak, dating from the end of the C15, was whitewashed over in the 1540s, thrown out in 1892, and speedily brought back after the Suffolk rain had revealed the treasure beneath the whitewash.

Depicting the drama of the Doom or Day of Judgement, the work would have originally been located beneath the chancel arch as the backdrop for the medieval Rood or crucifix with Mary, mother of Jesus and the Apostle John. It is now on the north wall to greet visitors as they enter the church through the south porch.

The two central panels show the righteous lining up in front of St Peter, also St Michael and the devil weighing a soul to determine its destiny. To the right are the gaping jaws of hell where the 'damned' are being dispatched. At the top are Christ in majesty, with his mother Mary and St John the Baptist to the right. The original colouring is simply remarkable.

Discover more...

- Holy water stoup or stone bowl at the porch door that traditionally would have contained holy water, blessed by a priest, for people to make the sign of the cross using the consecrated water, as an act of symbolic cleansing and rededication upon entering the sacred building
- Leman memorials of 1747 and 1757 flanking the east window. The Lemans were prominent in the church and the ring of six bells is attributed to them

95

THE MERRY WIDOW

Bridgett Applewhaite's ledger slab at Bramfield St Andrew IP19 9HT

Always look down as well as up in a church to see what is in the floor. Among the shiny black marble ledger slabs at St Andrew's you'll discover a fascinating example near the sanctuary step on your approach to the altar. It dramatically describes the demise of Bridgett Applewhaite, nee Nelson, in 1737, aged 44, who *'After the Fatigues of a Married Life, Born by her with Incredible Patience, For four Years and three Quarters bating three Weeks; And after the Enjoiment of the Glorious Freedom Of an Easy and Unblemish't Widowhood, For four Years and Upwards, She Refolved to run the Rifk of a Second Marriage-Bed.'*

Visit this fascinating church to find out what happened next. If you read the inscription aloud, you can get a real feeling for the attitudes of the time.

Discover more...

- The tower in the churchyard, the only round tower in England built detached from its church
- Beautifully worked 1400s roodscreen, described by author Henry Munro Cautley as 'the loveliest in Suffolk'
- Unusual C19 nave glass with remarkable floral designs by Constantine Woolnough of Framlingham
- The poignant figures in the chancel of Arthur and Elizabeth Coke with their baby daughter, sculpted in alabaster by Nicholas Stone. Dated 1634, it is thought to be one of the finest pieces of English sculpture of the period

JACK WHO STRIKES THE BELL

Jack-o-the-clock at Blythburgh Holy Trinity IP19 9LP

You will need to walk up the aisle of this vast and beautiful church on the Blyth estuary to encounter this fascinating little fellow in his sentry-box on the south side of the chancel. He wears armour of the mid 1500s, although some experts date him as late as the 1680s. His axe used to strike the bell on the hour, but now he announces the beginning of services.

Jacks are very rare, but this one has an older colleague in Southwold church dating from the Wars of the Roses.

On your way back down the aisle, look out for the figures on the bench ends representing the 'Seven Deadly Sins' of wrath, greed, sloth, pride, lust, envy and gluttony, as well as the seasons of the year.

Discover more...

- Devotional chapel in the little room above the porch
- Angel roof with original colour and mostly original angels
- Beautiful choir stalls with carvings of saints in their fronts
- John Hopton's 1478 tomb, which also served as the Easter sepulchre where the Sacrament was placed from Good Friday to Easter Day
- Dramatic 'Beast of Burden' sculpture in bronze under the east window by Laurence Edwards

97

A COMMUNITY WINDOW

Millennium glass at Uggeshall St Mary NR34 8BD

Scenes of village life surround the Virgin and Child in a stained glass roundel by renowned glassmaker and conservator Rachel Thomas, set into the perpendicular window nearest the porch.

Commissioned and financed by the villagers themselves to commemorate the Millennium, the scenes reflect life in the local community. Look carefully and you will see Red Poll cattle, sheep, bees and honey, spider's web and the Helio primrose, discovered and propagated in the village. The tiny tractor followed by seagulls is harder to spot. Can you find it?

Notice the teacup that represents the country teas that have been raising money for this much-loved building for more than 40 years.

Discover more...

- The elaborate Victorian reredos behind the altar, installed in the 1870s restoration and featuring eight saints against a gold background in C14 style
- Memorials to the Sheriffe family in the chancel. Harriet Sheriffe, daughter of clergyman Thomas Sheriffe who was incumbent at Uggeshall for 54 years, subscribed liberally to the Southwold lifeboats and the station's first self-righting lifeboat was named after her in 1852
- Walking out of the south porch, look directly ahead of you at the boundary wall and the gate through to the old rectory. If you look carefully, you can make out the remains of the text worked in knapped flint: 'Mark ye well her bulwarks...that ye may tell it to the generation following' from Psalm 48

A CHURCH WITHIN A CHURCH

The ruined church of Covehithe St Andrew NR34 7JW

The lofty tower of this church has served as both land and sea mark since the early 1300s. But when vicar William Yarmouth and his friends rebuilt the church on a massive scale in 1450, they could not have known that some 220 years later, it would become impossible for Covehithe's declining community to maintain it.

So in 1672, 28 years after William Dowsing had ordered the destruction of 250 pictures in stained glass, the parishioners partly dismantled the vast building and built the present tiny church within its ruins.

The drama of this mighty ruined church is heightened by its position near a rapidly eroding coastline.

Discover more...

- Two stones set in the chancel walls record the names of the churchwardens who 'put it out' – a reference to those who 'put out' the contract for the rebuilding in 1672
- Today's church incorporates C15 features from its predecessor, including the font, pulpit and a few salvaged poppyhead bench-ends

THE SAINT ON THE DOOR

C15 painting on rood loft stair door at South Cove St Laurence NR34 7JD

In many churches, you will see a mysterious staircase built into the thickness of the wall. Mysterious because it appears not to lead to anywhere in particular. In fact, such staircases provided access to the rood loft, enabling people to tend the many candles which burned in honour of the great Rood or Cross bearing the crucified Christ, flanked by his Mother and St John. Until their destruction in the 1540s, the Rood and loft were the focal point for the congregation in the nave.

At South Cove, not only the rood loft stair remains, but its original door bears an exquisite painting of the figure of St Michael completed around 1470. The work must have looked glorious when new, but although faded, the feathery archangel with his sword and the dragon at his feet can still be clearly seen.

Discover more...

- Two Norman doorways, the northern one containing a beautiful C15 door
- Medieval woodwork in the bench-ends, arch-braced roof and remaining part of the rood screen
- A banner stave locker built to contain the long staves or rods for processional banners, one of 26 in East Anglia

AN UNFORGETTABLE SCREEN

C15 painted rood screen at Southwold St Edmund IP18 6JA

Spanning the whole width of this magnificent church, the rood screen, once surmounted by the figure of the crucified Christ, is a prime example of the dazzling workmanship throughout this C15 showpiece of a building.

Dating from around 1480, the painted panelling at the base of the screen is its most eye-catching feature. The section facing the north aisle is of the Nine Orders of Angels under the Archangel Gabriel; the superb centre section is dedicated to the apostles, and the section facing the south aisle depicts the Old Testament prophets.

Every panel is in itself a medieval 'Old Master', designed as a visual aid for teaching Christianity to the C15 worshipper. The damage to the saints' faces is a reminder of how, in the early C17, the Puritans tried to wipe out all traces of such images, preferring to focus instead on Bible teaching from the pulpit.

Discover more...

- The grand exterior, elaborately decorated with patterns of knapped flint known as flint flushwork, contrasting dramatically with the white stone and the gleaming glass of the windows
- Vibrant C15 'wine glass' pulpit, rare to have survived the Reformation, perhaps due to the lack of obvious religious imagery
- Curious carved figures on the elbow rests of the choir stalls
- Southwold's Jack of the Clock, his armour dating from the Wars of the Roses, the period in which the church was built
- C20 east window depicting the elevation of St Edmund to sainthood, the last work of Sir Ninian Comper

A BRIEF GLOSSARY

Words commonly used for church architecture and furnishings

ALTAR/COMMUNION TABLE: The focal point of the church and traditionally in the sanctuary at the east end, although now sometimes placed nearer to the congregation. Here bread and wine are offered, consecrated and shared because Jesus asked that this should be done.

The service, which may be called the Holy Communion, the Lord's Supper, the Eucharist or the Mass, is one of the Sacraments, because Jesus instituted it and we often refer to the consecrated bread and wine as the Blessed Sacrament.

FONT: A receptacle, usually stone but occasionally wood or metal, to contain the water for baptism. It is usually placed near the main entrance to the church symbolising that baptism is the first step on the journey of faith.

LECTERN: A stand, with a sloping top and often in the form of an eagle, usually positioned at the front of the nave to support the Bible from which extracts are read during the service.

PARCLOSE SCREEN: A screen partitioning a side chapel or tomb from the rest of the building.

PISCINA: Usually found in the wall to the south of an altar and set within a canopied niche, this is a stone basin with a drain to convey the water used during Holy Communion into consecrated ground, and for rinsing the chalice used at the altar. Since 1300, the priest has 'reverently consumed' all consecrated material remaining after the Mass.

PULPIT: A raised structure from where the preacher delivers the sermon during a service, usually at the front of the nave, opposite the lectern.

REREDOS: An ornamental screen behind the altar.

ROOD/ROOD LOFT/ROOD SCREEN: Dividing the chancel from the nave and forming a beautifully carved and painted focal point for the congregation was the rood screen, giving a view into the chancel, above which was the loft (or balcony), approached by stairs in the wall and enabling people to tend the many candles which burned in honour of the great rood (the crucified Christ, with his mother the Blessed Virgin, and St John) which soared above it.

Roods and their lofts were destroyed in the mid 1500s, but some of the loft staircases and the screens (or parts of them) have survived.

SEDILIA: Decorated stone seats, often in lowered windowsills used by the celebrant of the Mass and his assistants and usually found on the south wall of the chancel.

CHURCH FLOOR PLAN

Look out for these features in your next visit to a church

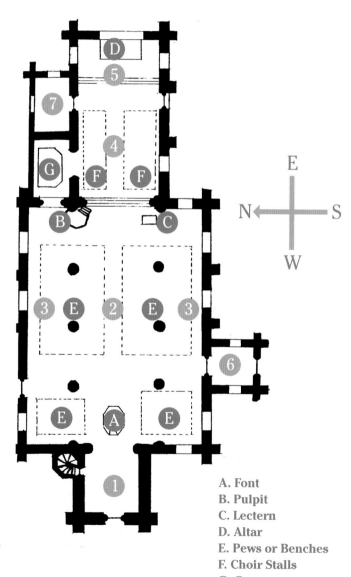

1. Tower
2. Nave
3. Aisles
4. Chancel
5. Sanctuary
6. Porch
7. Vestry

A. Font
B. Pulpit
C. Lectern
D. Altar
E. Pews or Benches
F. Choir Stalls
G. Organ

THANKS AND ACKNOWLEDGEMENTS

WORDS contributed by: Tim Allen, Diana Hunt, Roy Tricker, Marion Welham, Michael Wilde

EDITING: Marion Welham

DESIGNED and printed by: Anglia Print Ltd, a carbon neutral printing company

PICTURES: We are indebted to the following photographers who have given their services free of charge and without whom we would not have been able to produce this book.

Alan Bourne: 58
Chris Brookes: 5
Colin Canfield: 26, 41
Tim Crosbie: Page 8 and 27, 29, 49, 54, 59, 64, 71, 72, 74, 76, 78, 80, 81, 82, 85, 90, 91, 93, 97
James Halsall: 52
Dr James Harper: Page 2 and 60, 61, 63, 68, 69, 70, 73, 83, 84
Simon Knott: 10, 11, 16, 18, 19, 23, 24, 30, 32, 36, 39, 46, 62, 66, 92, 99
Iain McKillop: 6
David Stoddart: Back cover and 13, 75, 88
David Lamming: 22
David Offord: 42
Elliot Payne: Page 4
Misty Robson: 98
Norfolk Museums and Archaeology Service: 83 (Zeppelin in flight)
Spring Design and Advertising Ltd: 100
By kind permission of Thornham Parva St Mary: 40
The late Richard Tilbrook: pictures kindly donated by the Suffolk Historic Churches Trust: 8, 35, 37, 38, 55, 86, 94, 95
Christopher Tootal: 44, 45, 47, 48, 50, 51, 53, 56, 57, 87
Marion Welham: 2, 3, 14, 17, 25, 28, 31, 43, 65, 67, 77, 79, 89, 96
Michael Wilde: 1, 7, 9, 12, 15, 20, 21, 33, 34

Further reading

Guidebooks in individual churches
The Guide to Suffolk Churches, D.P. Mortlock, 2009
The Sutton Companion to Churches, Stephen Friar, 2003
Rice's Church Primer, Matthew Rice, 2013
The Buildings of England, Suffolk, by Nicholas Pevsner 1974
(Revision in progress by James Bettley for publication 2015)
Suffolk Churches and their Treasures, H. Munro Cautley (Currently out of print)

Useful websites

www.cofesuffolk.org
www.suffolkchurches.co.uk
www.angelsandpinnacles.org.uk
www.achurchnearyou.com (Churches' contact details)
www.shct.org.uk